A636

YOUR CAREER IN TEACHING

Teachers more than ever play a vital and valued role in modern society. The excitement of change and progress in teaching methods today is the keynote of this book about these highly skilled professionals, from elementary school through the university. This is also true of such closely allied occupations as school administration, librarianship, academic counseling, school social service work, overseas assignments, areas of specialization, etc. Fascinating case histories highlight the striking innovations taking place in schools countrywide, and focus on the scope of opportunities in a profession that offers stimulation and personal gratification.

YOUR CAREER IN TEACHING

BY

DOROTHY

AND

JOSEPH

DOWDELL

Illustrated with photographs

JULIAN MESSNER
NEW YORK

Printed in the United States of America
Library of Congress Catalog Card No. AC 67-10634

*This book is dedicated
with respect and affection to
Janet T. Snider,
an outstanding educator*

Acknowledgment

The authors wish to thank the following for their helpful cooperation in furnishing materials for this book: National Education Association, California State Department of Education, Sacramento State College, Stanford University, Sacramento City Unified School District, Bakersfield City School District, the Honorable Thomas H. Kuchel of the U.S. Senate, Delta Kappa Gamma, the Welch Scientific Company, Bausch & Lomb Company, Sacramento City College, San Juan Unified School District, and the American Seating Company.

The authors are most grateful to Mrs. Alex Snider, education consultant, for reading the manuscript and offering constructive criticism.

The authors wish to pay special tribute to Miss Bernice Braden, Librarian, Professional Library, Sacramento City Unified School District.

Contents

YOUR CAREER IN TEACHING

I

Take a Second Look

HELP WANTED: Superior young men and women needed
for important positions. Work vital to the future of
America. College education required. Good salary.
Rapid promotion. Fringe benefits. Box 899A.

What would you think if you saw the above advertisement
in your local newspaper? Would you assume perhaps that it
was from some new industry making special equipment for
space capsules? Or would you think that it was a government
agency seeking competent young people for a foreign assignment?

Please read the ad again. Then you'll realize that it could
just as well be an appeal for teachers. Superior young men
and women are needed as never before to teach the boys
and girls in our exploding population.

To get some idea of how fast the population is growing,
imagine yourself in the lobby of the Department of Commerce building in Washington, D.C. On the wall you will
see a huge electronic clock and a computer which is changing every few seconds to give the latest population figures.
The computer shows that there is one birth every 8½
seconds and one death every 17 seconds; one immigrant
enters every 1½ minutes, and one emigrant leaves every 23
minutes. There is a net population gain of one person every

13½ seconds, more than 6,400 every 24 hours, or about 2½ million every year.

In the 1960 census the population of the United States was slightly over 180 million. Now it is approaching the 200 million mark; and if present trends continue, there will be at least 250 million Americans by 1980 and 360 million by the year A.D. 2000.

Soon almost half of the population will be under twenty-five years of age. The fastest growing enterprise in America will be the education of all these young people. Imagine how many teachers will be needed! Teaching is already the largest of all professions; in fact, it is greater than the ministry, law, engineering and medicine combined. There is no end in sight for the need of good teachers.

Sometimes young people shrug off suggestions that they consider teaching as a profession with such remarks as, "I want to do something exciting!" or "I don't want to be stuck in a classroom, I want an important career." If they would take a second look at teaching, they would discover that it is one of the most vital, interesting and important of all professions. No other career offers more variety of activities; none provides more opportunity to be creative. Too, there are many inner rewards from teaching besides the salary earned. So let's take that second look and see if a career in education might not be right for you.

Your career in education would be beneficial to the country as a whole as well as to you. America cannot exist as a democracy unless its people are educated, not only to support themselves and live a richer life, but to make wise decisions about those who should govern and how the government should function. The founders of our nation, such as Thomas Jefferson, George Washington and James Madison, had the radical idea that a ruling class was not necessary because the common man could be educated to govern himself. So from the very beginning of our country right up to the present time, teachers have played an important role in making our democratic government and free enterprise system successful.

More than ever, good teachers are needed today to help young people cope with their rapidly changing lives. As the National Education Association reports, "Dynamic forces are working with incredible speed today. Man is advancing so rapidly that new knowledge and technology confront him before he has fully understood past achievements. Keeping abreast of developments requires running fast just to keep up. . . . The generation now in school will spend its adult years in a society as radically different from today's as the society of the sixties is from that of the early twentieth century."

Teachers help young people acquire a background of information so they can understand the forces and trends that will radically affect their lives.

Trends of today create the problems of tomorrow. For example, consider the trend toward urbanization. At the present time, seven out of every ten Americans live in cities. Already one sixth of the nation's population is squeezed into the supercity or megalopolis that extends from Norfolk, Virginia, up to Portland, Maine. Each year, more and more people crowd into the cities and make the problems of housing, water supply, transportation, waste disposal and crime control even more acute. Young people being trained in schools now will eventually find solutions to these problems.

Various forces are at work which will also present complex problems to the adults of the future. Some of these forces are the advancement of science and technology, especially in outer space; new methods of rapid transportation that will make our society even more mobile; the emergence of minority groups; the impact of mass media such as television; the extension of leisure time; and the shift of power among nations. The role of the teacher assumes more influence and stature in a time of such change.

Not everyone is aware that there has also been a knowledge explosion in recent years. It has been estimated that beginning with the birth of Christ, the first doubling of knowledge occurred in 1750, the second in 1900, the third in 1950, and the fourth only ten years later, 1960! Of course, new learning goes on all the time. To orient a child and to give him skills with which he can make use of even a fraction of this vast amount of knowledge will take a clever teacher, indeed. The role of the future teacher will be that of a guide through a wilderness of learning.

Are you the kind of person who likes a change of routine instead of being desk-bound? John Cranston, a young science teacher in a modern junior high school in California, is such a person, too. He likes the liveliness and variety of activities of his work.

John states, "There's never a dull moment! Something's going on all the time. Bells ring. Classes change. A new group of kids come in. Sure, I get tired and pushed out of shape sometimes but I'm never bored!"

The day begins for John when he signs in not later than 8:30 in the morning. Then his busy schedule on a typical day is as follows:

8:45– 9:35   First Period—Life Science or Biology, 9th
              Grade (an academically inclined group
              that John finds particularly challenging).
              Five minutes are allowed between periods.

9:40– 9:50	Home Room—John makes announcements about the student council meeting and a special assembly.
9:55–10:50	Second Period—General Science, 7th Grade.
10:55–11:55	Third Period—This is a preparation time for John which he uses to get special materials ready for brilliant students.
12:00– 1:00	Fourth Period—Life Science, 9th Grade (also an academically inclined group).
1:00– 1:30	Lunch.
1:35– 2:25	Fifth Period—General Science, 9th Grade.
2:30– 3:20	Sixth Period—General Science, 9th Grade.
3:20	School dismissed.
3:20– 3:40	Yard duty.
3:45– 5:00	Faculty meeting.

All levels of teaching offer a variety of activities. The teacher works with human beings, all with different personalities. No two classes are the same. No two days are ever alike.

In considering the advantages of teaching one should also be aware of the many opportunities there are to be creative in the classroom. Most people have a smattering of talent in many fields. No doubt you like to sing a little and have a slight artistic bent. Perhaps you enjoy writing poems or directing plays. Maybe you folk dance or read aloud with skill. If so, all to the good, as Judy Meyers, an attractive elementary teacher, found out.

As an indulged only child, Judy had been given years of music, dancing and art lessons. However, she was not good enough in any one talent to make a career of it. Sometimes her father, a successful businessman, would explode, "How are you going to earn a living with all this music and art? You'd better take some typing and shorthand."

But Judy passed up the business courses and went to college to train to be a primary teacher. Now she is teaching a first grade in the suburbs of a midwestern city. Her bulletin boards are among the most attractive in the school. She directs the primary choir which performs at school assemblies and P.T.A. meetings. Her boys and girls enjoy the folk dances she teaches them. Every bit of her talent and training is used to make her teaching successful.

Gary Knight, an English teacher in Maine, was made sponsor of the high school drama club. At first he was dismayed; then he discovered that he had a real talent for directing plays. Later he organized a Little Theater group in his community and derives hours of pleasure from it.

No matter how slight, whatever talents you have will be put to good use in the classroom. The chance to be creative is one of the most enjoyable phases of teaching.

The educational field has many facets. You can teach at any grade level from kindergarten through graduate school and in a dozen different areas. There are specialized subject fields, such as art, music or physical education. There are related fields such as in administration or guidance which offer opportunities outside the classroom. The field of education is so vast that you can find a career in it someplace to fit your particular needs and abilities.

Also, teaching is one of the few careers where you can "take it or leave it" and still come back. Girls, especially, should consider this advantage. Many young married women teach a year or two, then stop to raise a family. They might come back to teaching ten, fifteen or twenty years later. Their age will not keep them out of the classroom. Often young mothers, unable to teach full time, substitute several days a month. Others tutor in their homes. Teaching can be done on a full- or part-time basis, which can be most advantageous.

Education has long since opened its doors to all races. If you are a Negro, Puerto Rican, Oriental, Indian, Mexican or of any other minority group, do investigate what education has to offer you. You will find that your race is an asset and you will be sought after when your training is complete.

Dr. Blair Hurd, state coordinator of teacher recruitment, California State Department of Education, says, "The teaching profession offers countless opportunities to members' of all minority races. School districts across the nation, and particularly in California, actively recruit qualified men and women from all ethnic groups to teach in both elementary and secondary schools and in all professional specialties, including administrative and supervisory positions. I strongly urge college men and women of minority races who can qualify, to consider teaching as a career. These young men and women will enhance themselves in the teaching profession and make a major contribution to their country and to continued improvement in racial relations."

Teaching conditions are improving all of the time. Modern school plants provide pleasant working conditions. Salary schedules offer more remuneration each year and include many fringe benefits. Too, in many districts, staff members are entitled to a leave of absence for sickness, for family emergencies, for maternity, as well as sabbatical leave. Provision is made for retirement. Permanent tenure, which is granted after a period of successful employment, means that a teacher can only be dismissed from his position for causes specified by law on the basis of valid evidence.

However, you will find that the inner rewards of teaching are the most important of all. One of these inner rewards is the satisfaction that comes from doing purposeful work which benefits other people. To help a child master a new skill, gain insight into a problem and broaden his horizons is one of the most gratifying experiences a person can have. The teacher shares with the minister and doctor the opportunity to serve others and finds special meaning in his work.

Henry van Dyke, noted educator and minister, said of the teacher, "He communicates his own joy in learning and shares with boys and girls the best treasures of his mind. He lights many candles which in later years will shine back to cheer him. This is his reward."

Do you like to be around other people? If so, you will enjoy the other teachers and school personnel as well as the pupils in the classroom and on the school grounds. Teaching is an intensely social situation, and you will find your association with many people interesting and fun.

In most communities, teachers enjoy a certain prestige and are highly respected. It is true you will never be awarded a medal for teaching Johnny to read, but you will have status as being a valued public employee.

As a teacher you will be part of a large profession that is on the upgrade. Teaching is one of the first choices for careers, especially among high school honor students. As proof of the popularity of the field of education, approximately one third of all recipients of A.B. degrees every year are graduates of teacher-training programs.

One of the great inner rewards of teaching is the sense of being in the mainstream of life, not bypassed in some stagnant pool on the edge. In teaching you not only are earning a living but *are* living by doing something which is vital and worthwhile.

A secondary teacher, Sarah M. Bush, wrote, "My classroom is the theater of operations where I am the command-er-in-chief who leads his raw and inexperienced troops to wage unceasing war against the evil forces of ignorance and apathy. No day, no hour need be dull or routine where such an atmosphere prevails. I teach because it is the most exciting and most challenging life I can imagine."

So if you take a second look at a career in education you will find:

1. There is a great demand for teachers.
2. Teachers make a vital contribution to the welfare of their country.
3. Teaching offers a variety of activities.
4. Teachers have a chance to be creative.
5. There are many different positions to choose from in the field of teaching.
6. Teaching can be done on a full- or part-time basis.
7. Teaching offers countless opportunities to members of minority races.
8. Teaching conditions are improving each year.
9. Teaching is a popular profession.
10. Teaching offers many inner rewards.

Is teaching for you? Would any other field offer you more?

II

Schools for the Space Age

This is an exciting period in education. At last, schools are catching up with the space age. Changes are taking place so fast that school buildings can be obsolete as soon as they are built. Textbooks are out of date within months after they come off the press. New methods are replaced by still newer ones. University scholars, foundations, psychologists and visionary schoolmen are rapidly pushing out the frontiers of education. If a space camera were on a satellite over the United States it could record many unusual scenes in today's classrooms.

In a grade school in San Francisco, ten-year-old Debby sits in front of a computer attached to a typewriter. They carry on a lively interview. Debby types a message to the computer and then reads a response which comes back to her. Their interview goes like this:

Computer: "Hello. I am the Friendly Computer. Would you like to talk to me? Type yes or no, then press the key with R-S on it.

Debby quickly types "yes."

Computer: "Please type your name so I will know you."

The little girl types "Debby."

Computer: "I am glad to meet you, Debby. Can you answer this question? How many states are in the United States?"

Debby: "Fifty."

Computer: "Good for you. How many feet in a mile?"

Debby: "I think 5,280 feet."

Computer: "You're right. How long is one term of office for the President?"

Debby: "Five years."

Computer: "Sorry. Type again."

Debby: "Four."

Computer: "Very good, ring-a-ding. What is 8 × 7?"

In the Midwest two airplanes fly back and forth over six states. The planes carry transmitters which broadcast a total of seventy-two lessons a day over closed-circuit television to schools.

Chemistry classes in the high schools are watching a demonstration going on in a large university. A piece of magnesium is placed in an acid solution. The metal dissolves rapidly and a stream of hydrogen gas bubbles out. The professor explains that the hydrogen ion of acid bears a single charge of positive electricity.

While the chemistry classes are watching this demonstration, the elementary schools are having a lesson in social studies. On the television screens a noted historian is explaining the role the Mississippi River played in developing the Great Plains country.

This airborne teaching, called stratovision, is transmitted simultaneously over six UHF channels and covers subjects in all grade levels.

In a high school in Virginia a team of four teachers work together to conduct the English courses. While Mr. Rogers shows a film of Shakespeare's *Macbeth* to one hundred and eight pupils, Mrs. Cushing drills thirteen boys in grammar, Mr. Whiteside holds a staff meeting of the seven editors of the school paper, and Miss Long has ten boys and girls for remedial reading.

In New England, an experimental psychologist, Omar Khayyam Moore, carries on his studies to find out how very young children acquire complex symbolic skills. He analyzes how youngsters most readily learn to read, write and recognize numbers. His experimental methods motivate the child from within rather than by outside rewards or punishments. He calls this "autotelic learning." He is one of a group of psychologists and social scientists who advocate that the *learner* rather than the teacher should be the focal point in education.

In New York, an assistant director of school planning has a meeting with the members of an architect firm who are designing a new high school.

The director says, "This will be a big school. At least twenty-five hundred students. Let's find ways to break it down. Humanize it."

Leonard Hill, the senior architect, taps a pencil against his lips. "You mean decentralize it? We could divide the student body into five separate groups of five hundred each."

His associate, Elwood Carter, offers, "Each group could be an entity in itself. Have its own building, student body officers, and other activities."

A third architect points out, "All five groups could share the expensive facilities like the library, the cafeteria, the science labs and gymnasium."

The director nods. "Of course. But a student would spend

most of his time in his own smaller building, wouldn't he? There he would be an individual. Not just lost in a crowd. And above all, we must provide facilities for independent study."

The present revolution in education is causing drastic changes in at least three areas: (1) ways of teaching, (2) use of modern technology, (3) school planning. Emphasis on the individual to enhance the selfhood of each boy and girl is the basic principle behind all of these changes.

Ways of Teaching

The experiments conducted in the last few years by psychologists and social scientists have revealed that each child has an inner push or drive to become a more complete self. He wants to learn what is meaningful to him.

One psychologist advises the teachers, "Work with this inner push. Keep it alive and free. Stimulate it. Don't stifle it!"

Another has said, "Make the learner the base. Not the teacher. Not the subjects. Not the textbooks. The *learner.*"

A social scientist points out, "First you must understand your learner. Find out what his basic assets are. What he's up against. Develop positive self-attitudes."

Another adds, "You'll get a zest for learning when you develop a sense of inquiry. The very essence of education is *discovery.*"

A philosopher predicts, "These boys and girls are going to live out their lives in an entirely different world from ours. The knowledge we give them today may have no significance tomorrow. We must develop their inner resources, their ability to cope with change, and their creativity so they can find a place in their future world whatever it is."

However, once educators accepted the learner as the base and tried to enhance his individuality, they found that the old ways would not do. For example, it no longer worked to divide a group of boys and girls into grades according to their ages. A class of eight-year-olds could be on a dozen different learning levels. An eighth grade could have students ready for advanced high school work and others who could hardly do primary work. Some pupils can finish junior high school in two years while others need four.

A natural development of the modern philosophy of education is the nongraded school. In such a school, grades such as first, fifth or ninth no longer exist. Instead, the pupils are in one of four divisions: primary, intermediate, junior high or high school. Each division has a wide span of learning levels so that every child, from the gifted to the slow learner, can work to his capacity. Usually a pupil spends three years in each division. It may be necessary to spend more time, and some few will spend less time.

The pupil's abilities and characteristics are diagnosed before he is placed with an instructional group. The principal tries to place him with a teacher whose style of teaching will best suit him. Some pupils do better with a strict teacher. Others respond to a more relaxed atmosphere. The class usually includes children of three different age levels but who fit socially as a group. This is called "peer-group composition." Pupils should challenge each other but not be dominated by one or two overaggressive leaders.

It is the responsibility of the teacher of the nongraded class to select an appropriate task at the correct level of difficulty for each pupil. This does not mean a different lesson for all thirty children but an appropriate lesson for each one. Teachers are expected to teach each student where he is and take him as far as he can go comfortably and successfully.

A teacher can no longer complain, "His former teacher didn't cover division." If the pupil can't do simple division, that is where he starts. In every skill he works on his own level.

The goal is not to "cover" a certain amount of material. The pupil must really learn one step before he goes on to the next. He might start very slowly, then take giant strides.

Class placement is flexible. If a child is ready to move to another teacher on a different level at the end of three months, he is put there. He no longer waits to the end of the semester or year. If he has been placed incorrectly, he is changed to the proper group. In a nongraded school such terms as "being promoted" or "being put back" are obsolete.

A teacher in a nongraded school said recently, "We don't have the rigid floors and ceilings of expectation that exist in traditional schools. Boys and girls no longer experience failure. And they have to work hard to attain success. But they compete only with themselves."

The nongraded school is designed around the learner. The success of the nongraded movement has been dramatic, and pupils have made progress far beyond that which is possible in traditional schools.

Another outgrowth of modern educational philosophies is team teaching. This technique should not be confused with a departmentalized arrangement in which pupils move from one teacher to another.

Team teachers are *jointly* responsible for a distinct group of pupils. Together, the team plans, executes and evaluates the lessons.

For example, at Desert View Junior High School in Arizona, a team of three teachers are jointly responsible for all the students in general science. In September they met and planned the year's work together. They also divided the course into units.

At the initial meeting, Mr. Landus spoke up, "My major in college was chemistry, so I'll be responsible for all the units in that field. I can handle the physics, too."

Miss Butler nodded her head. "Of course, botany is my specialty. I'll be in charge of the work that deals with plant life. I can take care of the unit on bacteriology, too."

Mr. Fielding took notes of the planning, and then offered, "Leave the zoology and anatomy for me. I got my masters in 'Zoo,' you know."

Throughout the year they met once a week to evaluate the progress of their pupils, to make detailed plans, order science films and filmstrips, and make out tests. They had short, daily meetings to decide how to group their students and to co-ordinate last-minute details.

All of the pupils would meet together for the main lessons. Depending on the unit, Mr. Landus would conduct an experiment, or Mr. Fielding would use the skeleton to talk about bone structure or Miss Butler would discuss plant specimens. The large group would break up into smaller groups for review and study.

Sometimes Miss Butler would bring most of the students together to view a film. While she was with the large group, Mr. Fielding might be getting some special equipment set up for a demonstration. Mr. Landus could be in another room with a small group of pupils to prepare an exhibit for the science fair.

As a team, they gave their tests, corrected the papers and issued grades. Because they were a team, all of the students benefited by the special knowledge and skill of each teacher. By working together they kept up a high level of teaching.

While one had charge, the other two could "generate new steam." Each tried to do as well as the other two.

Some teams are organized differently. In Wisconsin, a typical team consists of two or more permanently certificated teachers (one of whom acts as leader), an intern teacher, and an aide or part-time clerical assistant.

An elementary school might have a team in which one member is the consultant in arithmetic, another in social studies and the third in science. An intern or student teacher might work on the team and be responsible for certain units and assist with the other work.

Team teaching has proved to be very effective, especially when the teams are well matched and special skills utilized. Of course, an incompetent instructor can do less harm if he or she is paired with strong teachers.

Another exciting procedure which is designed for the benefit of the individual learner is modular scheduling or, often called, flexible scheduling in the junior and senior high schools.

Educators asked themselves, "Is a rigid schedule the best? Should we always have exactly forty-five or fifty minutes for each class? Would we do a better job if we thought in terms of a week and let our daily schedule be flexible?"

In flexible scheduling the time is broken into modules of twenty minutes each. A teacher can request a single module or a long block of time consisting of several modules. He or she can request one or two students or several hundred. Instead of giving a lecture on Mark Twain five times to five different classes, an English teacher could call all of the students together at one time. He could give his lecture once and spend the other periods with small groups discussing and answering questions about the work of Mark Twain.

The homemaking teacher could have a long session for sewing twice a week instead of five shorter sessions. An art teacher might request her students for two hours to carry through a special project.

A teacher of a team plans the work and four days in advance submits a "job order," which is a request for time, particular students and facilities. A program coordinator works out the schedules on key-sort cards. The students themselves are involved in planning their schedules. Each day the student picks up his program card from his scheduling group teacher.

The flexible schedule allows time for the student to carry on independent study, and thus progress at his own rate. Teachers can have enough time to use imaginative procedures.

One of the first pilot programs, carried on at the Brookhurst Junior High School in Anaheim, California, revealed that flexible scheduling significantly improved academic achievement.

Programed texts are another new development. The material in a book is divided into "bite-size" units. After the pupil has studied the lesson he immediately uses a list of multiple-choice questions to check himself. Then he turns to the answer sheet at the back of the book to see if he has learned the lesson. If he has not, he studies some more.

The work in a programed text becomes an interesting game which involves the student and stimulates his zest for inquiry. A great deal of basic material can be learned this way which frees the teacher to spend his class time on pointing out the significant relationships in the material and drawing inferences and conclusions. Programed texts set the stage for sophisticated learning.

Use of Modern Technology

Education is the largest industry in the United States and involves at least one quarter of the population. More money is spent on education than in any other area except national defense. Yet this massive industry is only beginning to use modern technology.

"Isn't education a form of communication?" an electronics engineer asked. "Aren't you trying to get information from one source to another? If so, why don't you use modern equipment to do it?"

Many experiments and pilot studies have been conducted to find ways to use labor-saving devices to free teachers for more personal and specialized teaching. Educators predict that technological equipment will be used more and more in the future.

One principal stated, "Technology need not undermine good educational practices. It depends on how we use this equipment. Perhaps it will be the only way we can avoid regimentation."

Television is already used in the schools to enrich lessons and supplement teachers, but it is likely to play a far more important role in the future. The armed forces, industry, medical and dental schools have used television most effectively for training.

South Carolina has a state network which links all its schools into a huge installation. In this way the state is alleviating an acute shortage of teachers.

Advocates of television say, "We should use television in the areas that are beyond the scope of the average teacher—music, art, science and foreign languages."

Another says, "Isn't television a form of team teaching?

What difference does it make if all the participating members of a team are present or not?"

Some universities have circuit installations to share their top professors with their branches. By coaxial cable and microwave relays, their lectures are sent to campuses all over the state. Arrangements are made so that the students can ask questions.

Although the teacher will always be a valuable and necessary person in the classroom, there are areas in which television can vastly extend the pupil's educational experience.

Instructional films, slides and tapes are used extensively in schools. A new trend is the use of short single-concept films. These films are put on an 8 mm. cartridge projector. Students can use them in individual viewing booths in their independent study. Transparencies which are projected and synchronized with tape-recorded sound are another new teaching tool.

Teaching machines are valuable for individual instruction. These have reading pacers which the students adjust for themselves. The material is programed—that is, broken up into short lessons with questions—so that the student can constantly test himself. The programed material shows up on a lighted screen. There are machines that actually analyze a student's weak spots. Any necessary drill work can be learned more efficiently by the use of a machine than with a teacher.

With the use of machines the teacher's role will change and his time will be used in a more valuable and professional way. As B. F. Skinner, a pioneer in developing teaching machines, said, "Any teacher who can be replaced by a machine should be!"

Language laboratories, which have headsets so that a student can listen to tapes with recorded lessons in such areas as French, Spanish or German, have proved to be very effi-

cient. Then researchers asked, "Why confine listening laboratories to foreign languages?" Listening carrels are now built
in many modern schools and used in all phases of the curriculum. These carrels are equipped with headsets, micro-
phones and binaural tape recorders. The students listen, respond, record their answer and compare it with the correct
one. They progress at their own pace.

Computers will also be used extensively in schools of the
future. It is impossible to predict what new vistas will be
opened up in education through the use of computers.

Already administrators are using computers to build the
school schedule. Not only does the computer assign students
to classes, but it takes into account student and teacher pref-
erences, team teaching arrangements and flexible scheduling.
Data can be fed into the computer such as which teachers
are taking special training courses, what rooms are most
suitable for certain subjects, and what instructors have to be
"handled with kid gloves." Out of the computer comes a
master schedule that is far better than anything the most
conscientious principal can devise.

Computers are used for testing and analyzing students'
needs. They can give the teacher an itemized evaluation of
each student's work. Imagine how valuable a computer could
be to place pupils on correct learning levels in a nongraded
school! Experiments are being carried on to find ways of
using a computer in the learning process.

School Planning

"Education is on the move and the school building must
get out of the way," said Jonathan King, an expert on school
housing.

Flexibility is the keynote of modern education. Pupils

move from large groups to small seminars to independent study and back to large groups again. Television viewing, listening carrels and computerized learning will be part of the students' school day in the future.

The average egg-crate school, which is a series of boxes for classes of thirty pupils, is not flexible enough for Space Age learning. So new schools are being designed and old ones remodeled.

"Give us space for our fluid activities," educators plead. In response, school architects are designing open-space elementary schools for the new educational practices. These open-space schools have few interior partitions. Nor do they resemble egg crates. Some are built in a snail-like spiral; others have a cluster of buildings which are made up of a series of contiguous hexagons; still others are in circular pods.

Usually the equivalent of four ordinary classrooms is fused into one unit. In this space is housed four groups of children with their team of teachers.

When school opens in the morning the pupils gather in the large central space for opening exercises, and then report to their home station for attendance taking. Then they go to their proper group to work on their level of achievement in whatever subject is being taught. Throughout the day they are grouped and regrouped.

The trend in today's school is to cover most of the floor space with new, long-lasting carpet. It has been found that carpeting is more economical than maintaining vinyl tile floors. Carpeting deadens the sound and makes a room look like a library or living room rather than a kitchen. Certain areas which are used for arts and crafts are tiled. When it is necessary to partition off areas, movable chalkboards and portable storage units are used.

The new secondary schools provide for large group instruction, small group discussions and independent study. Here, too, the aim is flexibility, which is achieved through operable walls and movable partitions so that several small rooms can easily be turned into a large one or an open space partitioned off when desired.

The modern high school is designed to fully utilize television instruction, visual aids and other technological devices. Individual listening carrels and study booths are provided. A reference area has replaced the study hall. Teachers have office space near their classrooms.

New materials for construction have made a difference in school design. Geodesic domes, thin-shell concrete slabs, aluminum and plastic modulars have made radical changes in school housing. It is predicted that the trend will be toward curvilinear design, and many buildings will resemble an inverted umbrella with a column support in the middle.

As the country becomes more urbanized, planners foresee that schools and apartments will share the same structure. Playgrounds, gymnasiums and auditoriums will do double duty to serve the community as well as the school.

The revolution in our schools has had its impetus through massive financial support from both public and private sources. Behind many of the visionary changes are the Ford Foundation, Sloan Foundation, Carnegie Corporation and the U.S. Office of Education. The National Science Foundation, Physical Science Study Committee, and Educational Facilities Laboratories are also among the many forces at work. The most able brains in the country are planning new ways, new devices and new buildings to train today's children for tomorrow's world.

III

Is Teaching for You?

Have you ever asked yourself, "Would I make a good teacher?" Or "Would I like to be around youngsters all day?" Or "My grades are OK, but does it take a real brain to be a teacher?"

If you are thinking of teaching as a career, you have probably asked yourself these questions and a dozen more. You should do considerable self-probing and analyzing before you choose any career.

Before you can decide if you would make a good teacher you should know what factors contribute to successful teaching. To find out, let's review a principals' conference recently held at a large university in the Middle West. The theme of one of the round-table discussions was *Guidelines to Excellence in Education*. In this buzz session principals from all over the nation described the criteria they used in rating teachers' performance and what characteristics they looked for when hiring new members for their staffs.

A high school principal from New York, acting as group leader, began the discussion by saying, "A good teacher must have a sense of self-worth. He must have confidence in himself; otherwise he cannot gain the respect of pupils. I like a teacher who gives you the feeling that he really has something to offer."

"Empathy for others is important, too," a woman next to him suggested. "I want a teacher to be able to understand how people feel. Many children are sensitive, and they need to know that the teacher understands them and cares about them. My best teachers accept their children as they can and love them anyway. They might reject the children's actions, but they never reject the child."

Another added, "That's right. I always tell my teachers that it is the behavior you don't countenance—not the child. And along with 'empathy' I would like to put 'respect.' A good teacher respects a child's individuality as unique. He respects the child as a person. He respects him for his *innate* worth."

The group leader put in, "I certainly agree with you. Too many children have great potential which we do not always recognize. But a good teacher sees the child as he *can* be, not only as he *is*."

A grade school principal said, "Teachers should be warm and friendly. They shouldn't be standoffish with their pupils. 'Liking children' should not be a cliché but an actuality."

A junior college president from the West said, "I think a teacher's enthusiasm for his subject is most important. Enthusiasm is contagious. There's a meek little man on my staff who teaches astronomy. You hardly notice him around the campus, but his classes are always crowded. Once a month he holds an outdoor lecture at night and points out the constellations. People come from miles around to hear him. He is so enthusiastic about astronomy that you're spellbound listening to him."

A high school principal added, "I agree. Enthusiasm is important at all levels. Teachers must be salesmen. They have to be enthusiastic about something themselves in order to put it over."

"You're so right!" another high school principal burst in. "I tell my teachers that if they can't be enthusiastic about some aspect of their course, they should assign it for outside reading. Or program it. But don't stand in its way. It might prove interesting to the students—so let them discover it for themselves. Don't spoil it for them!"

An administrator from Ohio spoke up, "I stress leadership in teachers. A teacher must have well-defined objectives and the ability to guide a class toward these aims. It goes without saying that the teacher should have high personal standards and be a leader worthy of following. You know, for many young people the teacher is the best example they have to follow."

A principal from New England said, "No one has mentioned health. Teaching is hard, taxing work. A teacher should be physically healthy—emotionally healthy, too, I should add. The classroom is no place for the despondent or mentally ill person."

"Along with that," the group leader said, "you can put a sense of humor. A good teacher should have a sense of humor."

"Principals, too!" several added. Everyone laughed.

A junior high principal from Texas said, "I look for sincerity, or perhaps you'd call it 'dedication to the profession.' Too many girls think of teaching as merely a job until they find a husband—and yet they have the future of children in their hands! That is a tremendous responsibility. Give me the faculty member who sincerely wants to teach."

Someone spoke up, "It's not only some of the girls who are not dedicated enough. I've known men who have held down too many other jobs while teaching or have gone into politics or community affairs too deeply. I think a good teacher places teaching first."

"Creativity is important," another added. "A good teacher not only is creative himself but has the spark that develops creativity in others. Children waken in his room. He is willing to get off the beaten path. He provides the time and materials so that pupils can carry out their own ideas even if they differ from his."

A junior high principal from Florida put in, "Personality is important. A good teacher, like an actor or TV performer, needs to project himself. I want a teacher to have a real impact on his pupils."

The group leader added, "That's right. We've all noticed that our dull, uninteresting teachers have dull, uninterested pupils."

"Appearance is a factor to be considered, too," a woman insisted. "A good teacher doesn't have to be handsome or beautiful, but he or she should be neat and well-groomed. Well, more than that—they must look attractive."

"We mustn't forget that a good teacher has the skill to get the pupil and the material-to-be-learned together," a school superintendent said. "He is also able to evaluate what has been learned."

"I think respect for others is vital," an administrator from Oregon said, "and I mean respect in the largest sense of the word. A good teacher thinks of himself as a member of a team and should have a deep, abiding faith in group effort to solve problems."

"Isn't that the whole basis of democracy?" someone asked.

"Yes," the Oregonian answered. "Faith in the worthwhileness of others and willingness to work with others for a common goal are just as important in the teaching profession as in government."

The group leader put in, "Perhaps we could end this discussion by saying that a good teacher realizes the worth of teaching, too. He appreciates that he is part of a profession that is making a tremendous contribution to society."

From this buzz session one could make the following list:

A good teacher has—
  Confidence in himself
  Empathy for others
  Respect for a child's uniqueness
  Warmth and friendliness
  Understanding
  Enthusiasm
  Leadership
  Physical and emotional health
  Sense of humor
  Dedication to teaching
  Creativeness
  Interesting personality
  Pleasing appearance
  Skill to teach and evaluate
  Willingness to work in a team
  Respect for teaching

Before you say, "Wow! That let's me out!" remember that many of these qualities come with training and experience. Others can be developed with a sincere effort on your part. Of course, not all skillful teachers are strong in all areas. But one trait that all good teachers have in common is that they are deeply interested in the success of their pupils and work devotedly toward that end.

No doubt you've wondered, "Do I want to be around children all day?" That is a good question to ask yourself. But also ask, "Do I like people?" Remember that children are people—a bit younger and less mature than grownups, but people nonetheless. And very fascinating and interesting people, too!

Another question to ask yourself is, "Do I like to work and play with others, or do I honestly prefer being alone?" If you enjoy working with others, the chances are good that you will enjoy teaching. If you are a lone wolf, you'd better choose a more solitary profession, such as research or accounting.

While you are examining your interests you might also ask yourself, "Do people like me? Do they have confidence in me? Do they seem to enjoy working with me?" Remember that teaching is a two-way street. It is far more important for your students to like you and want to be around you than for you to like and want to be with them.

How can you find out whether you are suited to the teaching profession or not? Of course, aptitude tests are often helpful. College advisors can give direction to the older student. If you are still in high school you might talk with your principal or counselor. A teacher whom you respect can often give you good advice. An experienced educator can recognize qualities in you that would tend to make you a successful teacher.

Scholarship is important, for example. You must have college training before you are qualified to teach. Are you college material? But far more important than just your grades is an enjoyment of learning. In other words, do you like to study? Do new ideas interest you? Do you like to share these ideas with others? You might have ordinary grades but a great love of learning. Teaching is a constant state of learning and sharing.

A sense of responsibilty is a trait that all of your teachers will recognize in you. Do you usually get your homework in on time? Or are you always Alibi Andy? "Gosh, I had my theme all finished but it blew out of the car on the way to school!" "Honest, I finished that algebra assignment but my kid brother tore it up!" "Sure, I did that report but I must've lost it!" And what about your extracurricular activities? Do you forget committee meetings? Do you get dropped from the football team because you don't show up for practice? Teachers must have a sense of responsibility. If that is one of your weak points, you will need to strengthen it before you can become an educator.

A sense of responsibility is a trait that all of your teachers guide for your aptitude for teaching. A teacher must organize his semester's work, his units, his daily lesson plans. He must organize his time and his efforts. Are you disorganized? Are you always late? Do you spend too much of your studying time on your favorite subject and somehow never get around to your other assignments? If so, you'd better work on becoming better organized before going into the field of education.

Compassion is a trait that your teachers soon sense. Do you care what happens to your friends? What happens in your neighborhood? In your nation? In the world? Or are you completely self-centered? Teaching is not the profession for the "I'm only interested in me" person.

Leadership shows up in the very young child. Your teachers can sense it in you. Leadership is far more than being the Big Wheel who always gets chosen as team captain or elected to a class office. Leadership encompasses self-confidence, the firm but pleasant voice, the ability to express ideas, the capacity to take command or exercise authority when necessary. It is a trait which can be developed. Naturally the teacher has to stand in front of a class and lead it in the right direction.

Your capabilities or talents will give your advisor a clue as to your aptitude for teaching. *Webster's Dictionary* defines talent, among other things, as, "The abilities, powers, and gifts bestowed upon a man; natural endowments." So you see that "talent" has a broader connotation than being musical or artistic. For example, you might have the ability to think on your feet and give an excellent impromptu talk. This is a talent, too. You might have an analytical mind and be able to get to the basic concept of a lesson. Or perhaps you have mechanical or manipulatory ability. You may be gifted as an artist, musician, actor or writer. Whatever talents you have will enhance your teaching performance just as they do your student life.

For years people have had many misconceptions about teaching. Maybe you have made remarks about your teachers, such as: "Mrs. Livingston is married and has three children so, of course, she understands kids." Or, "Men make much better teachers than women." "Mr. Henderson's taught for twenty years, so, of course, he's the best in the Math Department." "Did you know that Miss White made Phi Beta Kappa in college? No wonder she's such a good teacher."

Extensive research was conducted to see what effect the following factors—intelligence, sex, experience, background, marital status and knowledge of subject matter—had on teaching success. There were some surprised educators when the findings were published. It was conclusively proven that many factors previously thought to be very important had little effect. To illustrate:

1. *Intelligence.* A teacher has to be intelligent, of course. But differences in intelligence have little effect on teaching performance. Whether a teacher's IQ rating is superior, very superior, or gifted is unimportant as far as his teaching ability is concerned. The fact that he made Phi Beta Kappa in

college does not insure his teaching success, either. Grades in college, even in teacher-training courses, matter little in the classroom. So take heart—even if you're not a "brain" you can still become an excellent teacher if you have other things going for you.

2. *Sex.* The researchers reported that whether a teacher is a man or woman makes little difference insofar as competence is concerned. So men are not necessarily better teachers than women. On the other hand, women are not always the best in certain levels, such as the primary grades, either. Both men and women should teach wherever they can do the best job—anywhere from kindergarten up.

3. *Experience.* Just how important is experience? When a teacher has taught ten years is he twice as competent as he was when he had taught five years? How about twenty years? Is he then four times better?

"No!" says the researcher. "A teacher becomes more effective for each of the first five years, and after that, he or she levels off." For most teachers it seems to make little difference whether they have taught ten years or fifteen or twenty.

One time a teacher applied for a job and with obvious pride declared, "I've had ten years' experience in the fourth grade!"

The superintendent asked, "Have you really had *ten* years' experience? Or one year's experience repeated ten times?"

4. *Background.* A broad background is helpful in teaching. But there is no substantial evidence to prove that a cultural background or a certain socioeconomic status helps to make a teacher successful. Fine teachers come from all walks of life and from all ethnic groups. Unsuccessful ones, too.

5. *Marital status.* The fact that a person is or is not married seems to have little bearing on his success as a teacher. Years ago it was common practice to dismiss a woman

teacher when she got married. Some school administrators felt she would no longer devote enough time and interest to her teaching job. Of course, the thousands of married women who are teaching successfully today have proved how invalid that theory was. Today over 75 percent of the women teachers are or have been married. However, the fact that a teacher is married or even has children seems to have little to do with his competency, according to recent research.

6. *Knowledge of subject matter*. It is often assumed that the more the teacher knows about a subject the more his pupils will learn about it. This is not necessarily so, according to the research conclusions.

Certainly at the college level, professors are usually authorities in their field. But it is not always the most learned professor in a department who is most successful in putting the material across.

Teachers on other levels often learn something along with their students in a most stimulating way to all concerned. Even the most highly informed person cannot make you learn. Learning is a do-it-yourself process. The teacher can only organize the material and set up the situation so that learning can take place.

Perhaps you have asked yourself, "How can I learn about boys and girls of different ages?" Or "How can I find out if they'll take to me?"

Perhaps you have family friends or relatives who are teachers and will let you observe their classes. Such an opportunity would be invaluable to help you decide what area of teaching you would like best.

There are many ways to have some "tryouts" with different age groups. You might assist some Sunday School teachers. A job as a playground director for a city recreation department is an excellent preteaching test.

A young man might be a Scout leader, do volunteer work at the Y, or act as Little League coach. He would also learn about youngsters if he umpired some softball games. Perhaps, too, he can put on a demonstration for a 4-H Club. Working as a counselor for a summer camp is also good training prior to teaching.

Girls who babysit with school-age children gain some understanding of boys and girls. Young women can often be counselors at Girl Scout or Campfire Girls camps. Sometimes girls can be library assistants and work with youngsters.

In many high schools and colleges there are branches of the Future Teachers of America sponsored by the National Education Association. This organization arranges field trips to schools, provides information about the teaching field, and often has educators speak at its meetings.

Have you heard your friends say, "I'm going into teaching so I can have a long summer vacation." Or "Teachers have a snap—they're through by three-thirty."

Have no illusions about the profession—teaching is hard work. It is a satisfying, wonderful profession but a most demanding one.

Teachers average thirty-five hours per week in school. At least ten hours more per week are devoted to work outside the school. The regular school year runs approximately 180 teaching days, which covers about nine and a half months. Also the trend today is toward longer days and all-year schools. So don't consider teaching if you are looking for a "snap" job.

What do teachers do besides teach? They spend hours of time planning and preparing for their classes. Surprisingly enough, the better the teacher the more time he spends in preparation.

Also, teachers must correct papers, keep records and make out reports. There are many meetings, in-service training courses and workshops to attend. A good teacher gives guidance and individual attention after school to students who need it. Parent conferences are an important phase of a teacher's professional work. Also many teachers sponsor the extracurricular activities of the school. A teacher's life is a full one, indeed!

Now that you know more about the factors that contribute to professional excellence, the aptitudes that tend to make successful teachers and the demands made on educators, you will have to decide for yourself if teaching is for you.

An educator once summed it up by saying, "You need a sense of wonder, a sense of purpose and a sense of humor."

IV

Time Out for Training

Before you can enter the teaching profession, you must qualify for a certificate or credential. Perhaps you think that these documents are issued on a national basis by some federal agency or authority within the profession. Well, nothing could be further from the truth!

Each state has full jurisdiction over its own schools under the provisions of the Constitution of the United States. Since the founding of our country, this state authority over public schools has been a jealously guarded privilege and was one of the controversial issues that brought about the passage of the Bill of Rights. Therefore there is not one but *fifty* different sets of requirements for certification, since each state has set up its own. No two are the same.

Of course, you are not likely to teach in more than one or two states, so you need not be concerned with all the requirements of all the states. You need only consider those in the states in which you seek employment.

Each state government issues certificates to those persons who qualify, permitting them to teach in that particular state. Certain colleges and universities are authorized by the state government to train teachers and recommend them for certification. Some states issue a few standard certificates with certain endorsements, while other states issue as many as sixty different ones.

The requirements for certificates change from time to time, too. A lawmaker may pronounce to the state legislature, "Teachers should know more about our state history!" and then propose a bill to that effect. Another might declare, "Teachers should pass a test on the U.S. Constitution!" and bring about a further change in requirements. Other government agencies might endorse more academic work or knowledge of visual aids or certain training courses. Sometimes the whole procedure becomes so cumbersome that the state has to completely overhaul it and start anew.

However, the process of certification serves many important purposes. First of all, it insures that children and youth will be taught by qualified personnel who have completed a program of preparation. It disqualifies undesirable applicants and weeds out morally unfit persons. Also important, it prevents misassigning teachers, such as forcing a high school teacher to take over an elementary grade, or putting a secondary teacher in a department in which he is not prepared —for example, an English teacher in a science course.

If you decide to train to be a teacher you will have to choose a college or university, either public or private, with a school of education. Some colleges include teacher training in upper division, while others offer it only as graduate work.

In the majority of colleges you can still major in education and obtain an elementary credential along with an A.B. degree within four years. Also, there are a few teachers' colleges that offer a two-year course for elementary teaching, but these are rapidly changing over to the four-year course. However, the trend is toward a five-year period of preparation—an A.B. plus a year of education courses for elementary as well as secondary certificates.

Each institution chooses its teacher candidates carefully.

Usually you must have a certain grade point average to qualify. Then you will be given an aptitude test. Not all people are psychologically suited for teaching and would do better in another profession. This aptitude test tends to disclose those who have made an unwise choice. Also you might have a personal interview with one or more professors in the education department. Once you have passed all of these hurdles you are ready to begin your training. Usually you will find that your school requires courses beyond those defined by the state government.

Perhaps you wonder what you must do to qualify for the various certificates. As an example of requirements for an elementary school certificate, those of the state of Illinois follow. In that state, the standard elementary certificate is valid for four years and qualifies one to teach from kindergarten through ninth grade.

To be granted an Illinois elementary certificate, the applicant must have an A.B. degree. The degree and credential can be earned within four years. The training is as follows:

General Education .... 38 semester hours
    Science .... 6 hours
    Social Science .... 6 hours
    Humanities .... 6 hours
    Health and Physical Education .... 3 hours
    Language Arts .... 8 hours
    Electives in above and/or Psychology.... 9 hours

Professional Education .... 16 hours
    Educational Psychology, including
        human growth and development .... 2 hours
    Methods and Techniques of
        Elementary Teaching .... 2 hours
    History and/or Philosophy of Education 2 hours
    Methods of Teaching Reading .... 2 hours
    Student Teaching grades K–9 .... 5 hours

Electives from above fields and/or
    Guidance, Tests and Measurements,
    and Instructional Materials .... 3 hours

Preparation in Methods for Elementary
    Teaching .... 36 hours

    This work must include methods in lan-
    guage arts, science, social science, music,
    art and mathematics

Electives .... 26 hours

                                          120 hours

Many states grant a provisional certificate to the beginning teacher. A permanent or professional one is issued only after the teacher has successfully taught a certain number of years. Some states require graduate study in addition to experience for the professional certificate. An example is Texas, which requires an approved graduate program of thirty semester hours plus three years' experience before a teacher may advance from a provisional to a professional certificate.

Another state that issues probationary certificates to beginning teachers is Vermont. To change to a professional certificate, an applicant in that state must have two years' teaching experience plus a recommendation from the last superintendent.

To teach in a secondary school in Vermont, the instructor must hold a high school standard certificate (probationary at first and then professional). The requirements for this certificate are:

    Bachelor's degree from an approved institution and a
        major in a high school teaching field.
    At least eighteen semester hours of professional training
        in five of the following areas:

1. Overview of Education
2. History and Philosophy of Education
3. Psychology of Education or Learning
4. Understanding the Individual
5. Methods of Teaching (required)
6. Observation and Student Teaching (six semester hours required)

In making a study of requirements in various states you will run on to certain terms that are frequently used and which may or may not be synonymous.

Let's start out with some easy ones. "Baccalaureate and Bachelor's" both refer to the A.B. degree. "Certificate" and "credential" mean the same. "Permanent" and "professional," in regard to certificates, are usually similar. However, Iowa has a "professional" certificate valid for ten years and a "permanent professional" one good for life.

The term "provisional" is the most confusing of all. You have already learned that a "provisional" or "probationary" certificate in many states is the initial one granted after full training. After a designated period of successful teaching the certificate is reissued as "professional," "standard" or "permanent."

However, in many other states, Idaho, for one, a provisional certificate is issued during emergencies for a limited time to those who have less training than is required for a regular credential. On the other hand, in the state of New York a provisional certificate is valid for five years and is equivalent to a standard certificate in the majority of states. To obtain a permanent certificate in New York State you must have completed an extra graduate year for elementary; on the secondary level, an additional fifteen hours in your teaching field along with six extra hours of professional training is required.

It sounds complicated, doesn't it? Well, it is. With fifty states changing, adding on to and subtracting from requirements for teachers' certificates, you might come up with almost anything. But you don't have to worry. Your school of education will be organized to abide by the regulations of the state in which it is located. You will have advisors who will make sure that you fulfill the necessary requirements.

But, you might ask, "What if I move out of my state? Will my certificate be good in another part of the country?" The answer is, "No." You will have to apply to the state department of education in the new locality and abide by its requirements in order to get a teaching credential.

In most instances, your training will be accepted in another state at full value. However, there are often special requirements for that particular state, and you may find yourself attending summer school to fulfill them. To illustrate, Wisconsin requires courses in conservation of natural resources for its science and social studies teachers and courses in cooperative marketing and consumers' cooperatives for some other teachers. Texas calls for a three-hour course in the federal and state constitutions for all teachers, which must be taken at a Texas college or university. It now takes five years of college training to obtain a credential in California. Too, many states differ as to what constitutes a teaching major for high school. Usually an out-of-state teacher will be issued some type of temporary certificate permitting him to teach until he can meet the special requirements.

If you move out of your state, it is important to have been graduated from an accredited institution. No less than fifteen states specify that the applicant must have an A.B. degree from an accredited institution. For example, Indiana requires "a baccalaureate degree from an accredited institution, and a recommendation from said institution." Other states use the term "approved" or "recognized."

So what is meant by "accredited"? It means that the school has been examined and approved by a team of educators. There are six regional associations throughout the United States (New England, Middle States, Southern, North Central, Northwest and Western) which require that certain high standards of education be met and maintained by all of the member colleges. A team of educators selected from the various regional associations visit the high schools and colleges in their area and carefully examine the programs offered. If the team appraise the situation (faculty, courses, physical plant, etc.) favorably, then the institution is listed as being "accredited." The accreditation system makes it possible for colleges and universities to accept the credits of high school students and transfers from other colleges at full value.

A voluntary agency known as the National Council for the Accreditation of Teacher Education (NCATE) examines the teacher training schools. This agency accredits those institutions that meet the required standards. The state agencies that issue certificates can evaluate the training program of an out-of-state applicant by seeing if it is approved by the regional association, or by NCATE, or by other professional commissions.

If you move from one state to another, you might have to take a proficiency examination in such subject areas as state history, constitution and health. Sometimes these examinations are in lieu of courses in these fields. Some states require a written examination to test all teachers of foreign languages.

In some states, a teacher who has passed an examination may move from one level to another. Too, in Utah, a holder of an elementary certificate may teach kindergarten by passing an examination. Other states hold written examinations for applicants for emergency or substandard provisional certificates.

There are many states that issue a "life" certificate which cannot be revoked except for moral reasons. In other states a "permanent" certificate remains valid only as long as the instructor teaches continuously or is not out of teaching beyond a specified number of years.

Some states issue a general high school certificate and then leave it up to the employing school to assign the teacher to his proper field. However, the majority of states issue a standard elementary or secondary certificate with necessary endorsements, which means that the teacher would be authorized to teach only in those fields in which he has had adequate training. Still other states issue separate certificates for each field.

So you see as long as there are fifty states you will find as many ways of certifying teachers. If you want to be further confused you can also inquire about regulations in the Virgin Islands, American Samoa, Guam, Puerto Rico and the Canal Zone!

However, there are certain trends in teacher training programs that will affect the educators of the future:

1. Many states are moving toward a five-year training program for teachers of all levels and specialities.
2. Ways to make it easier to employ out-of-state teachers are being investigated. Americans are mobile people. Teachers, too. Some authorities have suggested the use of a national teacher examination on top of an approved teacher education program to aid the state agencies. Others advocate that the teaching profession itself issue

a license to qualified teachers, which would be in addition to the state certificate.

3. The majority of states are scrutinizing their training requirements to adjust them to the dynamic changes in modern education. Schools are moving so fast that within a few years all teacher training is apt to be radically different from the present.

4. The emphasis in teacher training today is on an understanding of the learning process. Researchers are discovering how children actually learn, and these findings are affecting the methods courses taught in teacher-preparation programs. Courses in child and youth psychology and human growth and development are becoming more important, while many less meaningful courses are being dropped.

5. Teachers will be trained as clinical specialists to work in teams. Their role will be to guide the youth toward independent learning.

6. Teachers will devote more time to courses in their teaching fields so they will have a better understanding of what they are teaching.

7. Student teaching will play a greater role in preparation and will give the candidate a valid on-the-job experience. Internships will likely replace practice teaching. (The whole subject of student teaching is so important that the next chapter will be devoted to it.)

No doubt you have learned how important the state government, through its various agencies, is in the training of teachers. In fact, a teacher with an A.B. degree but only an emergency certificate might attend summer schools in various institutions and apply directly to the state for a standard credential. Her actual teaching would be accepted in lieu of practice teaching. She might never go through a regular teacher training program. However, you would find this a lengthy, roundabout way to achieve your goal.

Doubtless you will find your teacher training program a vital, worthwhile one. It will be your passport to a challenging professional life.

V

Sink or Swim

An important phase in your preparation to become a teacher will be your term of practice teaching. It no doubt will be the most dynamic, interesting and exhausting experience you ever have had. For the first time you will actually teach instead of just learning how it is done. You soon will find out what a great difference that is!

"For the first few days everything will be perfect," one education professor always warns his cadet teachers. "Then you'll make a mistake. Your supervising teacher will criticize you for it. Crash! Your world will fall apart! You'll lose faith in yourself. You won't be able to sleep or eat. You'll have a hard time pulling yourself together again. I'm warning you in advance so you'll be prepared for this mild manic-depressive cycle. You'll all go through it. But don't worry. It will pass and you will end up enjoying your experience."

There are more than 1,200 colleges and universities in the United States preparing teachers. Each institution has its own particular method of giving a candidate actual experience under the supervision of professionals. Each year more than 200,000 students are engaged in some form of practice teaching.

Student teaching may take up as little as one hour a day for four weeks to a full year as an intern teacher. Some institutions give as little as two hours of credit and others as many as sixteen units. Some cadet teachers are supervised by their college professor every day and others seldom see him. Some student teachers do little actual teaching, and others have the full responsibility of a class for a year and are paid a salary. Your experience in student teaching will depend on the policy of your college or university.

Many colleges and universities still use the traditional method of providing for student teaching. In this program the student working toward an elementary certificate usually takes practice teaching during his senior year, after completing most of his education courses. A candidate working toward a secondary credential has practice teaching during the fifth year of college. A professor in charge of the program arranges to have the student assigned to one or more master teachers in a school in the same city as the college. Nearly all colleges require twenty-four units of education courses, and practice teaching is one main part.

At first, the student teacher observes the class and the way the master teacher conducts the lessons. The student assists the master teacher in various ways. He might give tests and correct the papers. Often he will work with pupils who need individual help. Gradually he will take on some of the actual teaching. His supervising professor from his college will come to observe him and make suggestions. The master teacher will assist him all along the way.

Carol Mitchell, a slender, fair-haired girl, did her practice teaching in a fourth grade during her senior year in a college in the Northwest. For twelve weeks she worked under a master teacher, Mrs. London, who had supervised a number of student teachers.

"Mrs. London makes it look so easy," Carol thought to herself the first day. "But I know it's not."

For the first week Carol observed Mrs. London and got acquainted with the boys and girls in the class. Each day she took notes about the different pupils. She wrote:

> Tracy: a little beauty—should be on a magazine cover—won't play at recess for fear she'll get her dress dirty.
>
> Frankie: talks all the time—what a showoff—but how cute—I mustn't laugh at him any more, makes him worse.
>
> Doris: eyes frightened—cringed when I patted her on the shoulder—why?
>
> Bobby: big grin—proud of his Cub Scout uniform—promised to buy a Scout-o-Rama ticket from him—must remember to bring money.
>
> Manuel: ring of dirt around his neck—faded jeans—loves music—is on a free lunch program—eats as if this is the only meal he gets all day.
>
> Anna: tall for a nine-year-old—dress too short—very shy.
>
> Ronnie: leans forward when I speak—is he deaf?

During the second week, Carol had charge of a slow reading group and taught the spelling lesson to the entire class.

Carol wrote to her parents, "By the end of the day I am so tired I am numb! I can hardly drag myself out to my car. I don't know why. How will I ever teach all day?"

Her supervisor from the college, Professor Welch, came on Thursday to observe her teach spelling. All during the lesson Carol was so nervous that her knees shook, and it was all she could do to keep her voice quiet and pleasing. She knew she was hurrying too much. After the lesson she went with the professor to an empty classroom for a conference.

"Mrs. London is very pleased with you," the professor began. "She reports that you are most cooperative and have a pleasant way with the pupils." He placed an evaluation sheet on the desk in front of her and went on, "Your lesson was well prepared. It could have been effective. But you commenced before you had your pupils' attention. Then your pace was so fast that very few could move along with you."

"I know," Carol admitted. "I was scared to death."

Professor Welch smiled. "The first time is always the hardest." He made many suggestions to help her become more skillful.

Each week Carol assumed more responsibility. She initiated and carried out a unit on water resources. Arithmetic, music and art were added to her schedule. She kept on handling the spelling and her reading group. As time passed, she became adjusted to the busy day and felt more relaxed. Professor Welch observed her frequently so he could help her.

By the twelfth week, she was teaching all day. She was sorry when her practice teaching came to an end. The boys and girls gave her a farewell party on the last day of her teaching. She knew she would miss them all. Mrs. London wrote her a fine letter of recommendation.

Roger Wells was a student teacher in a junior high school on the East Coast. He was training to be a physical education and health teacher. He worked under three different teachers and gained technique from each one of them. He also helped coach the basketball and baseball teams.

His supervising professor approved of his work in the physical education classes, but he was less pleased with Roger's lessons in health. One of the evaluations read, "The general effectiveness of your lesson on communicable diseases was lost due to lack of structure in the discussion. I know you are trying to involve the students, and you may think that by allowing students to be casual and responding spontaneously, they will become more interested. However, this procedure of yours resulted in a completely opposite effect. Too many students tuned you out and paid no attention to you or the pupils who were participating in the discussion."

Roger had to work hard to improve his health lessons. His professor and master teacher made constructive suggestions about his procedures, and Roger tried to carry them out. Before the end of his stint he was doing well.

However, the traditional method of practice teaching is rapidly giving way to a newer, more dynamic approach called intern teaching. Internship is one aspect of today's revolution in education.

Ever since World War II, American schools have been under fire. Russia's early triumphs with Sputnik and putting a man in space brought on a wave of criticism of education in this nation. "What's wrong with us?" was heard from every direction. Too, the schools were bulging with students. After the war, the baby boom and the onslaught of veterans, who completed their education under the G.I. Bill, contributed to the crowded classrooms and shortages of teachers. The schools faced a serious crisis, and the need for change was in the air.

In 1951, the Fund for the Advancement of Education, which is part of the Ford Foundation, granted $85,000 to the University of Arkansas to conduct a statewide experiment in teacher training. A completely different, radical approach was to be tried.

The goals of the project were to give prospective teachers more time to learn the subjects they were to teach rather than how to teach them, to give the candidates a vital, first-hand teaching experience under close supervision, and to place more of the responsibility of teacher training on school districts.

Under this project, students spent their four undergraduate years concentrating on liberal arts courses in one of the fifteen Arkansas colleges and universities. During this time, they made no career commitments. Then they attended the University of Arkansas or Arkansas State Teachers College for a fifth year, which was devoted to teacher training. Along with enrolling in education courses, the candidates assumed the full responsibility of classes in the public schools as intern teachers and were paid for their services. College professors supervised their teaching. Also, an experienced teacher in each school was assigned to help the interns. This method was similar to the internship that is served by members of the medical profession.

The Arkansas project proved so successful that the Fund for the Advancement of Education has continued to grant vast sums of money to numerous educational institutions to further the development of the intern system.

The intern method is now accepted as a successful way of offering candidates valid teaching experience. In many areas this system is replacing the traditional practice teaching approach. Advocates of the newer method point out that the intern is accepted by the students and faculty members as a full-fledged teacher who will be a part of the school from the opening to the end of the term. Although the intern is supervised and guided, he must assume genuine responsibilities in his teaching. He then derives far greater benefit from the experience than if he were practicing at being a teacher.

Colleges and universities have modified the intern program in different ways. Many institutions now grant a master of arts degree on the completion of the program, but some do not. Some colleges have the candidates enroll in education courses during their upper division, and others concentrate all professional training during the fifth year. However, the various intern programs have many factors in common. The intern takes five years to complete the program. He acquires a broad general education as well as professional training. He is paid for teaching during his internship. He participates in a seminar in order to share his experiences with other interns.

Brian Hill, a student in a teachers college in the Midwest, took part in an interesting training program that covered a span of three years and which paid him a total of $4,500.

Beginning with his junior year, Brian spent one semester in college and one semester off campus as an intern teacher. During his first semester as an intern, he served as an aide on a mathematics teaching team in a junior high school in a city. He took roll, signed hall passes, gave tests and corrected papers. He had charge of the visual aids and was also responsible for the bulletin board displays. He supervised small groups of students who needed extra help.

The fall semester found Brian back on the campus as a senior. His program included such teacher training courses as educational psychology and child growth and development. These courses now had special meaning for him. He sought answers to the problems he had encountered while he was a teaching aide.

For his second assignment as an intern, Brian went to a small town at the far end of the state. He taught algebra and geometry under the supervision of a consultant from the county superintendent's office. The principal of the school also worked with him. His college advisor came only twice during the semester. However, the five classes in mathematics were his. Whether the boys and girls learned anything or not was his responsibility.

At first, everything went well. "It's just great!" he told his principal many times. He liked his pupils. He enjoyed the other members of the staff and made many new friends in the small town. But his high spirits didn't last long. By the end of three weeks things started to fall apart. His students weren't paying attention to him as they had at first. He began having discipline problems. Too many pupils made poor scores on progress tests.

"What am I doing wrong?" he asked the county consultant, Mr. Scribner, who had come to observe and confer with him.

Mr. Scribner took a ball-point pen and a notebook out of his pocket and then said, "A lot of things, Brian. But before we discuss them, let's see if we can get the principal in on this. Remember, he's here to help you. He'll have a lot more respect for you if you admit you are in trouble and ask him for his advice."

Brian, Mr. Scribner and the principal talked openly and frankly and tried to analyze what was causing the trouble. The three came to the following conclusions:

1. Brian did not start his lessons positively and clearly. His directions were too vague. He lost his pupils before he ever had their attention.
2. He created timing problems by letting the lesson drag on too long or allowing the students to divert him.
3. He was too friendly and too informal with his pupils.

"Brian, you're not in a popularity contest," Mr. Scribner stated. "You can assume that the boys and girls will like you. You need to make them *respect* you! You will gain their respect by being positive and businesslike."

The principal spoke up, "Don't get discouraged. You're young and inexperienced and you have to expect these slumps. The important thing is to do something about them before they get worse. I'll spend as much time as possible with you during the next few days and see how I can help you."

Brian worked overtime to have his lessons carefully planned. He wrote simple, clear directions on the board for each class. He dittoed suitable seatwork for those needing extra drill and planned challenging activities for his able learners. He adopted a more formal, professional manner.

Brian's positive actions and the principal's cooperation soon paid off. The students settled down to their work, and there were few discipline problems. Higher progress scores reflected the change in classroom atmosphere. Although Brian had his ups and downs during the remainder of the term, he never again got into such deep trouble.

When Brian returned to his campus in the fall, he took unusual interest in his courses on teaching methods. He looked for ways to prevent making mistakes in presenting his subject and in handling his pupils. Everything he now learned was meaningful to him. He particularly found the seminar helpful to him, in which all the interns discussed their problems and how to handle them.

When he was in his final semester of interning, which was in a junior high school near the college, he felt much more self-confident. Too, his professors were available for frequent consultation. By the time he had finished his internship and received a teaching certificate, he was a seasoned professional.

Nadine Leighton, a tall, attractive girl with auburn hair, was accepted in a typical intern program offered by a university in the West. The program was open only to those holding an A.B. degree and who had passed certain aptitude and achievement tests.

Upon completion of the program, Nadine received a master of arts degree in education and a secondary credential entitling her to teach her major and minor in a high school or junior college in her state. All during the year Nadine was enrolled in classes at the university as well as carrying on her teaching assignment, for which she received $1,800 pay.

At the beginning of the program, Nadine was required to spend the summer on the campus taking courses in education. Also included was experience in a teaching clinic. Each intern took turns teaching short lessons to a small group of students. The lessons were televised on a closed circuit to another room where the remaining interns and the supervising professor watched the procedure on a large set. With the guidance of the professor, the observing interns evaluated the lesson. The intern who was teaching was given a resumé of the evaluation at the conclusion of the lesson.

At first, Nadine felt self-conscious teaching under such circumstances. She said, "I'm sure I've made every mistake in the book. But at least I'm learning what *not* to do."

Soon, however, Nadine became accustomed to being "on stage" and was able to teach her lesson and take the evaluation quite objectively.

In the fall, Nadine was assigned to a team consisting of three interns and a master teacher. This team taught English in a high school near the university. Each intern member of the team was responsible for four lessons, which were observed by the supervising professor.

One of Nadine's lessons concerned William Faulkner. She used his story "Spotted Horses" as an example of his work. Although she had made careful preparation, the lesson did not go over very well.

In the seminar, following the lesson, she stated frankly, "I wasn't very good."

One of the interns spoke up, "Perhaps you overshot your mark. You kept talking about the viewpoint of the 'omniscient narrator' and the 'enveloping action' without first making sure that the students understood what you meant."

The professor said, "Excellent observation! Remember you must establish a common basis with your students so you can carry on a meaningful discussion." He smiled. "In other words, all of you have to be tuned in on the same channel."

Nadine nodded. "I see what you mean."

For the spring semester, Nadine was assigned to a high school about thirty miles from the university. She was one of three interns sent to the English department of the school. Each intern was fully responsible for two classes. Together the three interns took the place of one regular teacher who was on leave of absence.

An experienced teacher in the school, whose teaching load was limited to four classes, was designated as their resident supervisor. The university paid the school district for the time he spent with the interns. A professor from the university made many trips to the school to further direct the teaching of the interns.

Many times during the term, a camera crew from the university came in a special truck to tape the lessons taught by the interns. Later the tapes were shown in seminars to all the interns, who discussed and evaluated the procedures.

In no time the interns were able to pinpoint the flaws in their performance. As one of them said, "Our lessons are too teacher-centered. We all say 'Can you tell *me*' or 'I want you to study this lesson.' Or we answer the students' questions when four or five hands are raised."

Both the resident and university supervisor wrote out observation notes when they visited Nadine's class. Also they rated her on her aims, planning and performance. She was always given a copy of the observation evaluation sheet.

Some of the observation notes from the professor were quite formal. One read, "Nadine continues to develop strength in her planning. Much thoughtful preparation is in evidence. However, her students must become more aware of their own responsibilities in class activities that involve discussion and interaction."

The resident supervisor was more terse and to the point. For example, "Rattle their cages a little more! Look at their eyes. Be more specific with your illustrations. Relate your lessons to their lives."

The resident supervisor asked Nadine's students to write out what they thought about her strengths, weaknesses and how she could improve. These statements were typed out and given to her without the students' names. Some of them were:

Strengths

Miss Leighton is very pleasant toward the class. The discussions are interesting.

Students feel free to discuss any problems they have with Miss Leighton.

She explains the assignments fully.

She gets the students to answer their own questions during discussions. Applies the materials to the students themselves.

Her strengths are slight but good. I learn something but it could be better.

She goes along with the speed of the class.

She gets along with the students better than a lot of teachers I have had.

She goes kind of slow sometimes. She is a nice teacher.

Weaknesses

At times, she talks too soft.

Cannot make whole class participate in discussions, but what teacher can?

The class assignments do not coincide with our age level. We are in 11th grade and reading *Huck Finn!*

She backs down rather easily if you don't bring in an assignment; she says to bring it in tomorrow. This does give you a second chance to learn.

I think she teaches off the subject. I signed for English 5–6 not American Lit.!

When a person is called on, and doesn't know an answer, she keeps at it and asks more questions to him. Doesn't talk loud enough.

Improvements

Put the clamp down on students who interrupt the class.

She's doing a good job. It's me that should be trying to learn better.

Learn more about the ways of the students and not the standard method taught today at college.

Summarize the lesson when it's finished. Use graded papers to learn by and go over them in class.

Stay on the subject of English.

Be stricter on the subjects to be done at a certain time, and don't let anyone talk her out of it.

Nothing, I think that she is moving along at a rate that is not too fast and not too slow.

She should give us assignments we would enjoy doing.

Whatever your cadet experience proves to be, you will find it one of the most valuable phases of your training. You can find out what method of student teaching is offered in the colleges you are interested in by looking in their announcement of courses. Also, you can write to the dean of the school of education for information.

Here are a few tips to follow to make your student teaching more successful:

1. Devote yourself wholeheartedly to your teaching. Don't attempt too many other things such as holding down a part-time job or being involved in campus activities. Be professional in carrying out your responsibilities.

2. Try out your new ideas. This is the time to experiment, as you will have more expert advisors on call than at any other time in your career.

3. Make it your business to learn the names of your pupils, fellow teachers and the classified personnel as soon as possible, so you become an active part of the organization.

4. Prevent trouble. Do not leave your pupils unattended in the classroom. If you have yard duty be sure you are on the playground. Watch your temper so you are not guilty of sarcasm or striking your pupils.

5. Evaluate your progress and be receptive to supervision from your master teacher, your principal and college professor. Remember you are having the chance of a lifetime to learn from experts.

Your student teaching is a threshold to your profession. It is up to you to make it a vital, worthwhile experience.

VI

Help Wanted

As your training period draws to a close, you will naturally look forward to your first teaching position. You will have many decisions to make regarding your employment. You will ask yourself, "Should I teach in my hometown or in a strange place where I can meet new people and have different experiences?" "Do I want to live in a large city or a small town?" "What grade level do I want?"

Your college or university will no doubt have a placement bureau that will help you find employment. A college placement bureau has a double responsibility: to find positions for the graduates of its institution and to get the best possible teachers for the school districts it serves.

Before the bureau can process your application, you will be asked to compile material about yourself for your placement folder. This material will be available to superintendents and authorized school personnel officers. Of course, a copy of your scholastic record will go in the folder. You will have several data sheets to fill out about yourself which will also go in. These data sheets will have spaces where you will list your previous work experiences, your extracurricular activities, and any special abilities and interests you might have. A superintendent or personnel officer will study these very carefully, as he will want to find teachers who have had varied and broad experiences.

A superintendent will note with interest the section on work experiences. Your previous jobs, although they might have been menial, will have developed your sense of responsibility and your realistic attitudes toward employment. It will help you, for example, to have worked in a service station or in a recreation department. Perhaps you were a counselor in a scout camp, a farm laborer or a clerk in a store. Be sure to list these temporary jobs and include your employers' names and addresses, as well as dates of employment.

Extracurricular activities are important, too. Were you a reporter for the college newspaper? Did you go out for sports? Did you play in the band? Or were you on the rally committee? Perhaps you were an officer in a club or in the cast of a play. Whatever you did to show that you were a participator and not just an onlooker will add weight to your application.

Don't be unduly modest about your special abilities and interests either. If you folk dance, skin dive or water ski, put it down. If you play a musical instrument, sing a little or paint, don't be afraid to note it. Maybe you're a rock hound or cave explorer or have traveled a lot. Good! Remember that school administrators want teachers who have enthusiasms and hobbies. They want well-rounded employees with wide horizons. As one superintendent said, "I want teachers who are curious about their world."

One word of warning—take your time when you are filling out your data sheets. Use your *best* penmanship, grammar and spelling. Don't be like one young man who wrote, "I want to teach Chemestry and Pysics." "He won't in my school," said many a superintendent as they read over his folder.

One placement counselor wailed, "Why don't prospective teachers realize that these placement folders are speaking for them? When an employer sees a badly written, carelessly filled-out form he learns something about the applicant. He assumes that person will be equally careless and disorganized as a teacher."

You might be required to furnish a photograph for your dossier. It will pay you to have a professional photo taken in which you look your best. It is important to look like a mature person who is ready to hold down a responsible position. An extreme hair style or too casual clothes can spoil the impression you want to make.

You will also be asked to furnish letters of recommendation for your placement folder. These should be written by people who know you well enough to judge your ability to make a successful teacher. Your placement bureau may tell you how many letters to obtain. If not, try to get five letters.

One or two letters should be from supervising teachers during your interning or practice teaching. Perhaps the principal of the school where you did student teaching will write a letter for you. No doubt your college supervisor will furnish a letter. A letter from a minister in your home town as to your moral character will have value. A former employer who was pleased with your work could help you through a recommendation.

When you ask for letters of recommendation make it clear that they go directly to the placement office. The letters are confidential and you will not read them. Only authorized placement personnel or prospective employers will have access to them.

If you are asked what should go into these letters of recommendation, you could suggest that the writer's observations about the following would be pertinent:

1. Your sense of responsibility
2. How you get along with people
3. Your capacity for work
4. Your ability to adjust
5. Your appearance and grooming
6. Personality and character traits which will help you in teaching

If you write to a district superintendent, do address him by name. A "To whom it might concern" letter shows that you were too lazy to find out the hiring officer's name. The United States Office of Education puts out a bulletin, "Educational Directory, Part 2, County and City School Officers," which lists the county, district and city superintendents. Perhaps your college library has a copy. If not, send to the Superintendent of Documents, U.S. Government Printing Office, Washington 25, D.C., and enclose a quarter for your copy.

Remember that a letter to a superintendent speaks for you; so make sure that it is carefully written and worthy of an answer. If it isn't, it will be tossed into the waste basket.

For your letter use standard, 8½″ × 11″ business paper. The heading of your letter should include the superintendent's full name and title. The salutation would be "Dear Mr. Smith or Dear Superintendent Smith." Tell the superintendent why you wish to teach in his community and at what level. Give him a brief account of yourself, and tell him how he can get a copy of the credentials in your placement folder. Include a recent photo. Also enclose a self-addressed stamped envelope large enough to hold application forms he may want to send you.

It is during this application period that you should obtain as much information as you can about teaching opportunities. For example, you might wonder where the demand for teachers will be greatest in the next few years, geographically as well as on what level. Naturally the need for teachers will parallel the shifts in population. "You've got to go where the kids are," one placement counselor always advises.

It has been predicted that by 1980, 80 percent of the population will live in three supercity areas—between Bangor, Maine, and Norfolk, Virginia; Minneapolis to St. Louis; and from San Francisco to San Diego. If this prediction comes true, then the great majority of teachers will be needed in those areas.

At the present time there is an acute shortage of qualified teachers in the elementary grades. If present trends continue, there will be a shortage of nearly 25,000 qualified elementary teachers each year for some time to come.

Some high school fields, such as boys' physical education and social studies, have more applicants than there are openings. However, the acute shortage of science, mathematics and foreign language teachers continues to exist. There is always a demand for special teachers for the handicapped pupils.

Administrators, counselors and supervisors will be in demand at all levels for some time to come. Special personnel for the new teaching media—television, teaching machines and computerized learning—will have to be trained. Teachers on the college level will continue to be in short supply for several years ahead. Private schools as well as public schools will need staff members.

When you are considering various teaching opportunities, you should also look into positions with the federal and state governments. For example, the U.S. Bureau of Indian Affairs hires teachers for their Indian Schools. These are located on reservations throughout the continental United States as well as in Alaska. The Prison Bureau needs teachers for classes in its correctional institutions. State governments have openings for teachers in various institutions.

The time to have different teaching experiences is during the first few years of your teaching career. Then you can make changes without too great a salary adjustment. Often you are free of marital responsibilities, so you can venture out.

Perhaps you have always lived in a city and would like to try teaching in a small town or in a farming community when you begin your career. Consolidated rural districts frequently can match urban areas in salaries and working conditions. It will pay you to investigate them.

Maybe you will agree with a young man who recently received an M.A. degree from the University of California. "I have lived on the West Coast all my life," he said. "Now I am going to teach in a high school near Boston. I'd like to live in New England for a while."

Perhaps you know of a school district in a highly desirable area that has modern schools, excellent working conditions, and pays top salaries. You have heard that this district is deluged with applications from beginning teachers. You might keep this area in mind as your ultimate goal, but teach somewhere else first, and then apply as an experienced teacher.

As you gather information about teaching opportunities, you will also learn about salary schedules. You will find that most school districts operate under a single salary schedule. A single salary schedule is based on two factors—preparation and experience. This type of schedule does not take into consideration such factors as performance, grade level, marital status, dependents or sex.

A single salary schedule would look something like this:

Anytown Salary Schedule

Steps	Class I B.A. or less	Class II B.A. plus 12 units	Class III B.A. plus 24 units	Class IV B.A. plus 48 units or Master's	Class V Master's plus 24 units or B.A. plus 66 units
0	$5,350	$5,350	$5,600	$ 5,870	$ 6,160
1	5,400	5,600	5,870	6,160	6,470
2	5,600	5,870	6,160	6,470	6,800
3	5,870	6,160	6,470	6,800	7,150
4	6,160	6,470	6,800	7,150	7,520
5	6,470	6,800	7,150	7,520	7,910
6		7,150	7,520	7,910	8,320
7			7,910	8,320	8,750
8			8,320	8,750	9,200
9				9,200	9,670
10				9,670	10,160
11				10,160	10,670
12				10,670	11,200
13					11,750
14					12,320
15					12,910

In other words, if you were employed by Anytown School District you would receive the same pay regardless of whether you taught in elementary, junior high, high school or junior college. Every teacher in the district is placed on the schedule according to his experience and earned college units or degrees. The teacher with less training soon reaches his maximum and marks time, while the one with extensive training can work toward higher salary levels for many years.

You will find that under most single salary schedules, you

can get credit for only five years' experience outside of the district. In other words, a teacher coming into Anytown District on Class III with eight years' experience would have to start on Step 5 and not on Step 8. This means that as you stay in a district and climb up the schedule you may get to the point that you can't afford to leave. For this reason you should make your changes during your first five years, if possible.

Make it your business to find out about salary schedules on a nationwide basis. Perhaps your college library will have research bulletins with this information from the U.S. Office of Education and from the National Education Association.

As you look through these bulletins, you will notice that salaries for teachers are lower in the southern states than anywhere else in the United States. In one district in a southern state, the minimum is $3,215 per year. The maximum a teacher can get in the district, on the present schedule, even with an M.A. degree, is $4,169. Yet New York State has a law that teachers must have a beginning salary of at least $5,200. Massachusetts, Illinois and California are among the states with a legal minimum of $5,000, and the local districts often begin above that sum. Most districts throughout the United States pay the beginning teacher, with an A.B. degree, between $4,500 and $5,000. In many districts the maximums on the salary schedules go to $11,000 or $12,000, although some are much higher, for the classroom teacher with advanced training and experience.

When you are considering positions in different districts, look beyond the minimum on the salary schedules. Perhaps you will find that the increments or yearly increases are greater in one district, and you will soon be ahead. Some districts require professional growth, which means taking more college courses to remain or advance on the schedule. Others do not. Some have various steps that will reward you for higher degrees.

Some schedules have a maximum reached in a few years, and you mark time until the schedule is revised. Some give an extra $500 to the teacher who has been in the district for fifteen, twenty or twenty-five years. Some districts give merit pay for an exceptional teaching job. An example of merit pay would be a case in which two sixth-grade teachers with the same training and experience receive different salaries. The principal has rated one above the other in performance. The merit salary program is a controversial issue, with advocates on both sides.

When you have completed your placement file and have written your letters to various school superintendents (if you are going to), the next experience in line for you is the interview with your prospective employer. Some personnel officers visit the various campuses to conduct their interviews. Some ask the candidates to come to their offices.

If at all possible you should go to the district superintendent's office, even if it is some distance away. Then the interview will serve a two-way purpose. Not only will the hiring officer have an opportunity to talk with you personally, but you will have a chance to look over the school and the community to see if they appeal to you.

In some districts, a screening committee made up of members of the administrative staff will be in on the interview. In other cases, you will see only the superintendent or the director of personnel.

Do arrive in plenty of time for your interview so you can "pull yourself together." You want to give the impression that you are at ease, even if you aren't. It goes without saying that you should look your best.

The interview gives your prospective employer a chance

to judge you in many ways. He will ask himself various questions during the interview so he can later fill out a rating form on you. These questions will be similar to the following:

1. Does the candidate have a pleasing appearance? Is he or she appropriately dressed, neat, well-groomed and mature-looking?
2. Does the candidate show evidences of culture in speech and manner?
3. Is the candidate friendly?
4. Does the candidate have an air of self-confidence? Is he relaxed or ill-at-ease and overtense?
5. Does the candidate have a pleasant voice?
6. Can the candidate express himself well? Is he alert? Does he comprehend quickly? Does he have a sense of humor?
7. Does the candidate have recreational interests?
8. Does the candidate have desirable attitudes toward children and teaching? Is he negative? Eccentric? Biased?

You, too, should take advantage of the interview and get information. The interviewer will welcome questions from you for they will help him gain further insight into your professional attitudes. You should get information about the following points:

1. What your assignment will be if you are offered a contract. This will include the tentative school and grade level. (Most districts reserve the right to make changes in assignment.)
2. How many pupils you are likely to have in your class or classes.

3. How many teachers are in the school to which you might be assigned?

4. What the salary schedule is. The amount of yearly increments. What additional training is required? If any, what opportunities there are to take acceptable courses.

5. What the basic educational philosophy of the administration is. Is the philosophy modern with provisions made to use techniques such as nongrading and team teaching? Are visual aids used extensively? Are there pilot programs in force to find more effective ways to teach? On the other hand, is the philosophy very traditional? You must be able to concur happily with the philosophy of the school in which you work.

6. What extra duties and assignments are there beyond your classroom teaching? These will include sponsoring student activities, working on curriculum committees or child study programs.

7. When you are expected to report for duty.

8. What housing is available in the community?

9. What recreational facilities are in the community?

10. What the community expects of the teacher. Are teachers expected to participate in community activities? Attend church? Teach Sunday school? Are their private lives their own or subject to censure?

When the interview is over, you should certainly try to visit the school where you are likely to be assigned or at least a typical school in the district. Try to go when school is in session. Then you can meet the principal, talk to the office staff, meet some of the teachers and observe the children who come to the school. Certainly you will see what condition the school plant is in and have a realistic basis to decide about a job in the district.

When you are offered a contract, think about it carefully. Within a reasonable period of time either sign it or return it unsigned with your decision. Thus the superintendent will know where he stands in regard to his staff needs.

When you sign a contract, do so in good faith with every intention of living up to it. Refrain from seeking other positions. It is unethical to break a contract to accept a better job somewhere else. Contracts should be broken only under the most severe circumstances. A young man might be drafted. A woman's husband is transferred to another city. Accident or unforeseen illness prevents the signer from fulfilling his duties. These reasons would be considered legitimate ones. In some states your credential can be revoked for breaking a contract to accept another position.

It is important for a beginning teacher to get off to a good start. If you are moving to a new community, do so well before the beginning of the school year and get settled. Then prepare for the opening of school. The secret of a good start is not to attempt too much all at once.

Familiarize yourself with the course of study and curriculum guides of your particular assignment so you can begin the year with an air of self-confidence and having things under control. Do this well before the preschool workshops and meetings so you'll know what the supervisors are talking about. You are likely to be teaching courses or on a grade level in which you had no experience as a student teacher. You might have to reorganize your instructional materials.

Also before the opening of school you should prepare your room. This will include getting the necessary books and supplies on hand. You should arrange your bulletin boards and displays to have an interesting room environment. That important first week of school will also go much more smoothly if you have carefully made lesson plans and work sheets ready.

As a beginning teacher you will work under certain handicaps, such as being inexperienced and having to get adjusted to a new school, new faces and perhaps a new community. You will have to prove that you can teach successfully.

However, you will have many factors in your favor. It will pay you to take advantage of and capitalize on them. Some of them are:

1. *Enthusiasm.* A young, beginning teacher often brings wonderful enthusiasm and spark to a bunch of tired, battle-worn veterans. Enthusiasm, like good humor, is contagious. You might inject new life and renewed spirit into a jaded group. If you do, you will be forgiven a lot of mistakes you might make due to your inexperience. Be enthusiastic about your school, your class and teaching. Usually established teachers complain just to let off steam. But you haven't had time to build up excess steam and frustrations, so complaining is a privilege you haven't earned yet.

2. *Energy.* A young teacher is expected to be "in there pitching." Remember you have the energy to push the visual aid cart down the hall or to rush out onto the schoolground and settle the fight behind the backstop. You should be the one to fill in as the folkdance partner for the leftover youngster or to hunt up the missing child on the field trip. The veteran teacher is in there with the authoritative word and all the background information about a situation. At least you should contribute some brawn.

3. *Unblemished reputation.* The fact that you were hired for the job indicates that the administration thinks well of you. Of course, you have to prove that you are a good

teacher. But at least you've done nothing yet to show that you aren't. Most veteran teachers have made mistakes they have to live down—ones they would give anything to forget. You still have a clean slate.

4. *Cooperative attitude.* Every principal faces a certain amount of resistance to his directives on the part of his tenure teachers. Some veteran members of the faculty are rigid and not at all receptive to new ideas and new methods. No matter what it is, they're "agin" it. Some of them are prima donnas and have to be handled with extreme tact. Even so, they may not cooperate.

On the other hand, administrators expect full cooperation from the beginning teachers and will have no patience if they don't get it. So cooperate if it kills you! Be on time with reports. Be sure they are complete and accurate. Abide by school rules. Carry out orders cheerfully. Like all neophytes, you may get stuck with the unwanted job or the pupil who's a pest. Take these in your stride and know that someday you, too, can be more choosy.

5. *Receptive to supervision.* The beginning teacher, fresh from internship and college, is conditioned to supervision. He is used to being evaluated by his professors and fellow student teachers. He is resilient and can be directed. Remember that one of the most important responsibilities of your principal is supervision of his staff.

Your receptivity to your principal's constructive criticism and supervision can be one of your greatest assets. Work with him. Discuss your problems with him instead of covering them up. From the very beginning of education, every teacher has had problems—so he will expect you to have some, too. Naturally you will handle unimportant details yourself, but go to him with your big problems.

Seriously consider your principal's suggestions, and do something about them. If they don't work, tell him why *after* you have tried them. Be receptive. Let your principal feel that he has had a hand in your success.

You're off to a good start! Good luck!

VII

Try This on for Size

No doubt it has been some time since you attended grade school. When you are thinking about a career in education you are apt to give first consideration to teaching in high school or college because your experience here has been recent. But don't overlook the elementary level. This may be an excellent field for you.

If you could interview personnel directors in school districts across the nation you would hear them plead for elementary teachers. "We have too many applications for high school positions and not nearly enough for our elementary schools." "We want more men in the lower grades." "I wish more Negro men would train for elementary teaching." "Young people should go after elementary certificates. There is always a need on that level."

An estimated student population of some sixty million in the next decade will contribute to a large demand for teachers, especially in the elementary field, according to figures prepared by the U.S. Office of Education.

A young man will find the elementary field a satisfying one as a career or as a steppingstone to administrative or supervisory positions. The elementary level is particularly suited for the girl who might marry and leave the profession for a considerable time to raise a family. When she returns to teaching, she will find it is easier to get an elementary position than any other. Also those living in rural or remote localities are more likely to find employment in elementary rather than secondary schools.

You learned in the preceding chapter that the vast majority of school districts operate under a single salary schedule, which means your pay in the elementary field would be the same as if your assignment were on the secondary level.

However, your best reason for choosing the elementary field would not be because of the many job opportunities nor the equable salary but because the area is a fascinating one in which to teach. You would be working with pupils who are in a particularly interesting stage of their development. It is certainly worth your while to investigate this branch of education.

Your experience as a teacher in a typical K–6 elementary school would be different in many ways from teaching in a junior or senior high school. Some of these differences are:

1. *Number of subjects covered.* A junior or senior high school teacher concentrates on one or two subject areas in his major and minor fields. A foreign language instructor might teach Spanish and Latin. Another might have science and mathematics. But an elementary teacher is responsible for many subjects, in some cases up to twelve, ranging all the way from spelling to science. If you have a wide range of interests, this variety of subjects will be one of the advantages of elementary teaching.

2. *Maturity of pupils.* The age span of the pupils in a K–6 school is twice as long as that of junior and senior high school students. The ages of the elementary youngsters through sixth grade would run roughly from four years nine months to twelve years.

Along with this wide span of chronological ages you would

find an even greater variation in maturity levels. Maturation includes many factors such as interest span, muscular co-ordination, readiness to learn, as well as emotional and personality development. Elementary children move rapidly from one stage to the next. They "grow up" before your eyes. You will find it most interesting to watch a youngster change from a small kindergartner to a subteen during his grade school years.

Because the learner in the elementary school is still child-like and immature, the methods of teaching should be suited to him. The atmosphere in the classroom is informal and the learning is centered around the child. On the other hand, the junior and senior high school instruction is more formal and subject-centered, since the pupil is ready for this.

3. *Relationships with students.* If you were to teach in a junior or senior high school you might have from 150 to 250 pupils per day. Although you would be vitally interested in their welfare, you might not know them too well, even by the end of the term. It is usually their counselor, the school nurse or attendance officer who is involved in their personal problems. The pupils, too, are quite self-sufficient.

On the other hand, as an elementary teacher you would be completely responsible for thirty to forty children who are still dependent on adults for direction. Even though you are on a teaching team or in a departmentalized situation, you will have your homeroom youngsters enough to know them intimately. Legally, you must be concerned with their manners, morals, safety, health and emotions as well as what they learn.

You will hear a lot about the "whole child" and this can mean everything from comforting him when he skins his knee or making sure he has a jacket on before going out in the cold to finding out if he understands long division. Your role in grade school is half-parent and half-teacher.

4. *Contact with parents.* As a teacher in a junior or senior high school, especially one located in a city, you are likely to have little contact with the parents of your students. There will be many whom you will never see. Those parents who do come to school usually deal with the counselors or principal.

On the other hand, as an elementary teacher, you are apt to know many of the parents. Many mothers and fathers are active in P.T.A. and youth groups such as Scouts and Little League which bring them to school. There are parent conferences and school functions that provide chances for you to know them. Usually an elementary school is much smaller than a high school and is located in the neighborhood, so parents find it easier to visit school. Too, younger pupils encourage their parents to be part of their school lives, while older boys and girls tend to discourage such participation.

5. *Learning goals.* As a high school teacher your main goal for your students would be that they gain an understanding of a subject that will enrich their lives and help prepare them for college or a vocation. However, in grade school, your goals would be somewhat different.

The three R's—so much a part of the elementary curriculum—are skills that must be learned. Time is set aside in grade school for this purpose. So along with informational subjects to cover, you will have the responsibility, as a teacher, of seeing to it that your pupils learn to read, write, spell and do arithmetic. Later, as these students progress up the educational ladder, they will have little time to spend on gaining proficiency in these basic skills.

If you enjoy being around young children under twelve, if you would like to teach a variety of subjects, if you would like to work closely with pupils and their parents, then teaching in the elementary field might well be best for you. Before you make a final decision, however, you should visit some typical classes at the various levels and see what is taking place.

Perhaps you will agree with Nancy Price that kindergarten is "tops." Nancy, who has taught for two years, is very proud of her kindergarten, which is housed in a separate building and has its own playground. Her room is a sunny cheerful one with plants in the window, goldfish swimming around in a lighted aquarium and a canary singing merrily in its cage. A bantam hen, in a pen in the corner, clucks softly.

Nancy has one class in the morning from 8:45 to 11:10 and another in the afternoon from 12:45 to 3:10. If you would visit her room about nine in the morning, you would find the class in an activity period. One group of girls might be playing house in the corner where there is a miniature stove, refrigerator, and cupboard with toy dishes and a small table and chairs. In another place a group of boys may be piling large hollow building blocks on top of each other. "They're always building a rocket to the moon," Nancy explains.

There are three easels with small pots of tempera paint and wide brushes ready. Nancy keeps several large sheets of newsprint thumbtacked to the easel. Each easel can accommodate two artists, so Nancy has made six green smocks for them to wear. The children take turns painting.

The rest of the boys and girls are seated at the tables assembling jigsaw puzzles or stringing large beads on plastic cords or coloring on newsprint with special wide crayons.

If you would ask Nancy what the boys and girls learn in kindergarten she would say, "You could say that kindergartners become conditioned for school. They adjust to a routine, get acquainted with the school grounds and buildings, and learn to obey school rules. Also these children learn to get along with other boys and girls—which is very important for the only child. They learn to obey school rules, too. They also learn to pay attention and follow directions, which are important for primary work."

She might think a minute and then go on, "They are building up a large oral vocabulary which gets them ready to read. The more they talk to each other and exchange ideas and broaden their experiences, the more of a foundation they will have for reading.

"They have lots of number readiness, too. Just knowing that it is time for recess or time to rest is a start toward telling time. Experiences like passing out two graham crackers or lining up by twos or being one of a group of six children painting at the easels or four in a sandbox at a time builds up a concept of number."

After you leave the kindergarten you would find it worthwhile to drop in on one of the first-level primary rooms in this nongraded school. Mrs. Bennett, an older woman, will tell you, "I'm afraid I'm prejudiced. I like primary and wouldn't want to teach anywhere else. I like to work with young children before they become too grown up. Besides, the most exciting experience you can have is teaching children to read."

While you are observing her class, Mrs. Bennett might help the boys and girls write an experience chart.

"Something very interesting happened today," Mrs. Bannett begins. "What was it?"

One little girl raises her hand. "Mr. Hanson brought a raccoon to school."

A boy speaks up, "He had it in a big cage."

A dozen hands go up. "He had a mask across his eyes." "His front paws look like hands." "He had a long nose."

After much discussion the boys and girls decide what is to go on the chart.

A Raccoon Visits School

Our custodian brought a raccoon to school in a big cage. He is tame. His name is Mask because he has a black mask across his eyes. He has a long nose. He likes soda pop and will hold the bottle with his hands.

Several boys and girls take turns reading the chart. Later, Mrs. Bennett will work with the slow readers and help them read the chart. Then the children draw a picture of the raccoon. You, no doubt, will agree that Mrs. Bennett's room is a busy, interesting place, where much learning is going on.

Before you leave the school you should stop in at one of the older classes. How large the pupils will look in comparison to the primary children!

These boys and girls are working on their unit on water conservation. Their desks are pushed into groups of four or five, so the various committee members can work together. One committee is working on watersheds. The pupils are looking in encyclopedias and other reference books for information.

Another committee is making a study of dams and reservoirs in the state. These students are using pamphlets from the state department of natural resources. Another group is examining maps that show the location of the rivers and lakes in the state. Still another group is planning to report on the uses of water. A low, orderly hum of voices is heard, indicating project activity is going on.

Their teacher will tell you, "They work in committees very well, for they have been doing it for some time. They set up their own standards of work, elect chairmen of committees and plan their projects with little confusion. We will visit the city filtration plant as a field trip and the pupils will carefully plan for that, too."

A study of the curriculum areas covered in the elementary program might help you gain an insight into this level. One of the most important curriculum areas is that of language arts, which enables the child to communicate with others. Language arts cover reading, spelling, handwriting, listening, creative writing, speaking, grammar or correct usage, literature and foreign languages.

Reading is the most important skill learned in the elementary school and is fundamental to all other subjects. "Reading is the key that unlocks the door to learning," one educator has said. "Both teachers and pupils spend more time and effort on reading than on any other subject."

Reading is a difficult skill to master. A careful foundation must be laid from kindergarten into first grade, just to build readiness for reading. A reading vocabulary is an outgrowth of a child's speaking vocabulary. Reading should begin with a child's life experiences. A teacher does this by writing experience charts with her pupils. After the charts, following in careful sequence are sentence strips, flash cards, preprimers, primers and finally readers.

You might hear a mother say, "I want Tommy to be able to express himself—to say what he means." This is a worthy goal for Tommy and all other children, for it has been estimated that more than 80 percent of all communication in the world is oral, in spite of all the books, magazines, letters and newspapers which are written each year. A vast number of people earn their living by speaking—salesmen, lawyers, ministers, teachers, business executives and actors, just to mention a few. Oral expression is an important part of the language program.

The elementary school offers the pupils different opportunities for oral expression through conversation, reporting, dramatic plays, choral speech and storytelling.

Spelling must be learned early, and more time is spent on spelling in elementary school than the average person realizes. A skilled teacher drills the children on the words they use frequently in their written work. She also tries to find ways which will interest a child so he will help himself to spell better. She encourages him to keep his own word list of "bugbears" in a booklet so he can refer to them when necessary.

Handwriting is also necessary to self-expression. The primary teacher introduces manuscript rather than cursive writing to the very young pupil for several reasons. Manuscript writing is easier to learn and gives a pupil the feeling of success. The letters look the same as those he learns in reading. Manuscript is less tiring to a child, as it requires less muscular and eye coordination. Cursive writing is usually introduced when the child is about eight years old.

The elementary child is given much experience in writing reports, themes, summaries and announcements. Correct English usage is emphasized. The teacher incorporates regular grammar lessons in the assignments. She encourages the pupil to proofread his work and correct any mistakes.

Foreign languages are now becoming a part of the curriculum in many elementary schools at about the fourth grade. The states in the West and Southwest emphasize Spanish because of their proximity to and the heritage from Mexico. On the other hand, the states close to eastern Canada offer French. A number of states teach German.

Parents and teachers alike agree that children should be taught to read well, speak clearly, listen attentively, spell accurately and write legibly. However, as everyone knows, this is no small order.

One of the most interesting areas in the curriculum is the social studies program. This includes history, geography and a study of contemporary life and its social problems. The goal for the program is to produce informed, responsible, self-directing citizens. Such citizenry will in turn improve group living not only in the classroom but eventually in the community, the nation and the world.

The framework for the program, which provides a sequence, expands with the child's widening interests. In the primary grades, the child begins with the home, the school and the neighborhood. Then a city community and a rural community will be studied. Usually a primitive civilization such as Indians, Pueblo Indians or Eskimos will get some attention. The first part of the intermediate level might be devoted to a study of the state. Colonial America and the westward movement and modern America often will be the program for fifth graders. The next step of instruction will be a study of North and South America and the Pacific. The seventh grade will consider other parts of the world, and the eighth grade will usually study the United States Constitution and government.

However, there is nothing rigid about the framework. Often the program is carried on in a series of core units in which the class is interested. Such central problems as "What effect does urbanization have on America?" or "What role did the Mississippi River play in developing the Midwest?" or "How have the forests helped our country?" afford a big scope to the program, although they do not necessarily fit into any particular grade level. The pupils break the main

problems down into smaller ones, and they work in committees to assemble the information into reports. All subjects,
such as art, music, science, language and arithmetic, are involved in some way in the unit work.

Much of our modern civilization is based on the achievements of mathematicians. The spectacular exploits in space,
the expanding use of computers and the new industrial discoveries are only a few of the feats of those skilled in mathematics and engineering. A real understanding of arithmetical
principles is necessary. Elementary teachers have the responsibility of establishing the groundwork in understanding
modern mathematics. It is a challenge that proves the importance of elementary education.

Exploring the natural environment through a study of science is another interesting curriculum area. Many teachers
who do not have a real desire or background to study pure
science in depth often thoroughly enjoy the simple and more
practical aspects of science covered in the elementary level.

One fourth-grade teacher remarked, "No one could be less
'scientific' than I am. Yet I worked with my class on a unit
in electricity. For the first time I learned that the terms
volts, amperes and ohms were named after people. By the
time we were through the unit, I really understood many
facts about electricity and found them fascinating."

Health and physical education is another important area
in the curriculum. Studies in this field help to develop the
child and carry over into adult life. The child from a culturally deprived home may have his only training in good
health habits and nutrition while in school. Physical education in elementary school often creates a lifetime interest in
sports.

The fine arts field offers the child many creative experiences. Singing, listening to music and playing in a band not

only enrich the child's life but lead to greater interests in adulthood. All types of arts and crafts motivate a child toward self-expression and appreciation of the beautiful things in his world.

In the broadest sense, the term curriculum means every experience a child has in school, both on the playground and in the classroom. Watching the custodian repair the drinking fountain, eating in the cafeteria, taking part in a school program, are all part of the elementary curriculum. The goal of this curriculum is to develop the child and prepare him for his future school and adult life.

"What characteristics make a good elementary teacher?" you might ask. The same characteristics that make a skilled teacher at any level contribute to success in the elementary grades. Intelligence, enthusiasm, thorough training, dedication and understanding of children are a few of these qualities.

However, there are particular personality traits and abilities which have special significance on the elementary level. To mention some of them:

1. *Patience.* To help a small child learn new skills requires patience and time. It has been estimated that a child has to have seventy experiences in a new concept before it is part of his permanent learning. The elementary field, especially in the primary grades, is no place for the nervous, high-strung, sharp-tongued teacher.

2. *Warm personality.* The teacher who has warmth, who is outgoing and compassionate should be in the elementary classroom. The small child may feel somewhat insecure away from home and need reassurance from his teacher.

3. *Smattering of talent and broad interests.* It is far more important for the elementary teacher to have a little talent in many areas than to be truly gifted. The fine, highly trained

musician or artist, the dedicated scientist and the outstanding mathematician belong in the secondary field. The elementary teacher is fortunate indeed if she can carry a tune, play the piano a bit and folk dance. He or she should "know a little about a lot."

Now that you have reviewed the elementary field you might desire to find your professional niche there. If you do, you will make an important contribution to education, and you will be in for the adventure of your life.

VIII

Adolescents in Abundance

In the warm May sunshine the new John F. Kennedy High School looked opulent and serene in its quiet suburban setting. In front of the main building, the sprinklers made a row of miniature fountains across the lush green lawn. A blackbird darted down from a branch of a Douglas fir tree, tiptoed across the grass and stood in the spray. Three cars were parked in the "visitors only" spaces near the front entrance. No one was in sight.

From the exterior, the high school seemed strangely tranquil when you knew some 1,500 teen-agers were inside. But once you pushed open the heavy glass door and walked past the bronze bust of the late President and on into the main corridor, you could almost feel the vitality and pulsing life of the school.

In a large-group presentation room, three teachers had 120 students assembled from their Social Studies IV classes. Mr. Stegner, the teaching team leader, began, "We will make plans today for our field trip to the state capitol. Let's have some discussion."

A dozen hands were raised. Mr. Stegner looked at a red-haired boy. "All right, Bob."

"We ought to decide what is our purpose for the trip. Of course, I know we're going to learn about our state government in action. But shouldn't we decide on a list of questions we want answered?"

"Very good, Bob." He turned to the blackboard and wrote "1. Purpose for the field trip." "We'll come back to this point later."

He thought to himself, "This has been a good class. I'll miss them next year."

Then he called on a girl. "Shouldn't we set up our standards for the trip?"

"Indeed we should, Debby." Mr. Stegner wrote "2. Standards for trip." "Wally, can you add to our list?"

"You should put 'People we want to see.' We ought to talk to the governor if we can. There are a lot of others."

A girl spoke up. "We'll have to have a committee to write for appointments with these state officials."

In the homemaking wing, Miss Warren surveyed the line of girls against the back of the room. She said, "This is our last rehearsal before the fashion show, so everything must be in readiness. Becky, did you fix that hem in your formal?"

When Becky answered in the affirmative, Miss Warren turned to another girl, "I see that you took care of that puckered seam, Ann."

She examined each girl and then said, "You all look like fashion models. You're just lovely." She was desperately tired and her head pounded. But in spite of that, she wondered if anything could be more satisfying than helping girls learn to sew. It was so worthwhile. These girls would use sewing long after they had forgotten their other high school subjects, she told herself.

In the music room, Mrs. Wilkins stood in front of the choir. "Let's try that last stanza again. Altos, you must come right in on that F sharp. You're too slow! Remember, you must come in more quickly. It's only two weeks before the music festival, so we have to work hard!" She heard her voice rise with tension.

But, as she directed them, she thought to herself, "Really, they sing like angels!" Their voices were so clear and true that shivers ran down her spine. She had to blink hard for a minute to stop sudden tears.

John F. Kennedy High School is an interesting place, but perhaps no more so than any of the other 28,000 secondary schools in the United States. About twenty million young people are enrolled in our junior and senior high schools in grades seven to twelve. For many of these young men and women, senior high school is preparatory to college. However, for approximately two thirds of the students, high school may be the last institution of learning they will attend.

The secondary schools are designed to meet the needs of young people at a crucial time of their lives when they are no longer children but still not quite adults. It is a period when many adolescents seek emancipation from parental control. Adolescents reach their adult levels in intelligence. Social life and status are important to young people in this period. Too, an adolescent wants to learn new skills and move rapidly to the independence of adulthood.

An elementary child is satisfied with just one or a small group of teachers at a time. But junior and senior high school students, as a rule, much prefer moving from one instructor to the next. A secondary pupil has reached such an adult level of achievement that he cannot be limited in instruction. He is ready for experts in many subjects. His self-sufficiency and need for independence makes him rebel from the constant direction and supervision so necessary to the younger child.

Over 600,000 teachers are employed in junior and senior high schools of the United States. Perhaps this field is the right one for you. In order to qualify for training for the secondary level, you must have good grades and a real interest in the teaching field. In most states you will have to devote a fifth year to graduate work to receive your secondary certificate.

As an example of requirements for a secondary certificate you might consider the recommendations of the Northwest Association of Secondary and Higher Schools. These recommendations include:

1. An A.B. or higher degree from an accredited college or university. Teachers of special subjects who meet the requirement of states are considered eligible.
2. A minimum of fourteen hours of professional training, which must include educational psychology, methods and practice teaching.
3. A minimum of sixteen semester hours in the teaching field. Each subject taught must have six hours of college preparation except science, which requires eight. Teaching fields are social studies, science, mathematics, foreign language, home economics, language arts, business education, health and physical education, agriculture, art, music and industrial arts.
4. Core teachers must have twenty-four semester hours appropriately distributed among core subjects. Driver education is approved in the states in which it is taught.

The North Central Association of Colleges and Secondary Schools has similar recommendations except that the semester hours required for the teaching field and for professional education courses must each total eighteen hours.

The training of teachers is one criterion used in rating high schools by regional accrediting associations, so their recommendations carry weight in setting up state requirements. However, it is well to check the standards in your particular state to make sure you qualify in all respects for your secondary certificate.

It is also well to remember that not all majors in college are teaching fields in high school. If you major in engineering, astronomy or Russian, to name a few fields, you would not qualify as a candidate for high school teaching.

In deciding on a teaching field you should consider the special areas as well as the general ones. There is always a demand for teachers in such specialities as industrial arts, homemaking or fine arts. Also teachers of agriculture are valuable members of the staff and are sought after.

Vocational training courses make a major contribution to the education of the high school students who do not go on to college. Courses in business, auto mechanics, printing and drafting are only a few that prepare youth for useful lives. You might be the right person for a position in one of these areas. But be true to yourself and choose the field that is of greatest interest to you.

You should have two teaching fields to offer your employer. Frequently a high school teacher must teach in more than one area. So both your major and minor in college should be in subjects that are taught in high school. Perhaps an English major could have a minor in history. A music major might have a minor in a foreign language. A physical education major could have a minor in science.

Having "two irons in the fire" not only prepares you for more flexibility in assignment as a teacher, but also provides you with breadth of scholarship and intellectual attainment. A broad cultural and liberal education is very important in secondary teaching. Not only does a teacher instruct in his field, but he also bears the responsibility of passing on the culture and values of society.

The world is changing so fast that during your career you may be teaching subjects unknown today. You must gain facility in gathering valid information, in evaluating results and in coming to logical conclusions. The more complex society becomes, the more difficult it is to exercise discerning judgment, to know what is relevant or to decide what course of action to pursue. A liberal education becomes more essential in this period of social upheaval.

Such opportunities as travel or experience as an exchange student will be most advantageous in your teacher preparation. In your choice of elective courses, you should select those that will provide you with insights into man's activities. Such courses may prove to be the most valuable ones you've had before you complete your life as a teacher.

You have learned that a liberal education and specialized training in your field are essential. Don't underestimate the value of your professional courses in teacher education. There is a wide chasm between having knowledge yourself and having the ability of passing it on to others. Too, good classroom management is important to learn. Your professional training will provide you with skills, insights, competencies and attitudes that will help make you a successful junior or senior high school teacher.

Your education courses will cover the history and philosophy of education, the purposes and objectives of secondary school, and the nature of human growth and adolescent development. Modern teacher preparation stresses the psychology of learning and its place in curriculum planning.

You will be given opportunities through interning or practice teaching to learn techniques of classroom management and methods of teaching your subject.

Aside from all the preparation for secondary teaching there are certain personality traits and attitudes that make some teachers of adolescents more successful than others. Some of these are:

1. *Decisiveness.* Junior and senior high school students like to know definitely what is expected of them. The teacher who makes assignments that are clearly understood, and who is resolute and businesslike, is the one who has the best classroom management. The teacher who is vague and unsure of himself is in for trouble.

2. *Commands respect.* Along with decisiveness, a teacher who has self-confidence and inner security is likely to gain the respect of his students. His firm stride as he walks into the room, the way he stands with his head high, his strong voice which can be heard throughout the room, all add to his "presence." A teacher must project a forceful image.

3. *Fairness.* Adolescents have a keen sense of justice and are quick to resent unfairness. They feel that they have been "picked on" or that a teacher "has it in" for them. It is important for a teacher to gain a reputation for fair play and impartiality.

4. *Positive attitudes.* The teacher who is convinced that the vast majority of adolescents are well-behaved and co-operative is more likely to succeed at the secondary level than the one who is always expecting trouble. A teacher should also have respect for his profession and believe in the worthwhileness of teaching. The negative-thinking person— one who is overcritical—should earn his living some other way.

5. *Imaginative teaching.* The teacher who can lift the les-

sons out of the humdrum has gone a long way toward putting the material over. No one gets bored more easily than an adolescent. The enthusiastic, creative teacher, who can relate the learning to the life of a student, is bound to be successful.

Television programs, books and movies have sometimes distorted the role of the teacher. Some young people enter the profession with unrealistic aims and a fairy-tale picture of their ability to help their pupils. There are certain pitfalls that you should avoid when you become a teacher.

Barbara Neff was a competent teacher who taught history in a high school in an apple-growing district. One fall, when she gave a mental maturity test to her homeroom pupils, she found that Ralph, a junior, scored very high. He was placed in an individualized study program under her supervision for part of his work.

During one of their conference periods she said, "By Christmas you will be ready for the Civil War period. We will—"

Ralph spoke up, "Oh, I won't be here then."

Miss Neff was appalled. "You don't mean that you're moving? Why, you're just getting started!"

Ralph shrugged, "I never stay anyplace very long. My folks pick fruit. We're here for the apples. Then we'll head south for the citrus crop."

"Why, that's awful! They can't do that to you!" Miss Neff's voice was shrill with disapproval. "You are a gifted boy! You should stay in one place and go to school."

Ralph slumped down in his desk and had little to say for the rest of the conference. He could hardly keep his mind on his studies. For the first time he was really ashamed of his folks. And he had been so proud of the new truck and the long house trailer that they had been able to buy. But now he didn't think much of them.

"We're fruit tramps, that's all. Just a bunch of crummy fruit tramps," he told himself. "I'm going to tell the old man so. Not that he'll do anything different."

Miss Neff never knew what harm she had done. She had destroyed Ralph's self-esteem and disoriented a close-knit family relationship and had given him nothing in its place.

Perhaps someday you might become very upset if an underprivileged boy comes to school with a bruised face and black eye. You just know that his father has beaten him again. However, the boy might secretly respect his father and would resent outside interference.

If you become a teacher in a high school be very wary of showing disapproval of subcultures. You will soon find out you cannot play God and solve all the problems of youth in the lower socioeconomic level. In many cases the family life is functioning reasonably well as it is. You may rush in and cause havoc, where a highly trained social worker or counselor would proceed most cautiously.

Phil Hudson was a handsome junior high school teacher, and more than one of his girl students had a crush on him. He should have ignored this attention, knowing it was a harmless phase that the girls were going through before they found real boy friends of their own age. Instead, he encouraged their hero-worship because he found it very gratifying to his ego. He didn't realize that one of the girls was emotionally unstable. She was not able always to discern between reality and dream fantasies. One day he was called into the principal's office and confronted with a hysterical girl and her parents.

"I've never touched the girl," he said over and over.

It wasn't until the girl finally confessed she had "made it all up" that he felt he was safely out of a sticky situation.

The attractive young woman teacher who allows herself to be flattered by her boy students, and the man instructor who plays up to the girls, can let themselves in for trouble. Keep your relationships with your students on a professional level so you can help them in appropriate ways.

Frances Reed was never accused of being anything but hard-working and dedicated. However, she was known to be a tough teacher in her English classes. "What a slave driver!" or "Man, does she pour it on!" were common reactions to her overlong assignments and hard tests.

She spent hours meticulously correcting her pupils' homework. If anyone were to accuse her of competing for homework time, she would vehemently deny it. But it was true. She had an unconscious urge to prove to herself and others that her class was the important one. Avoid this pitfall and be satisfied with a fair share of your pupils' study time.

Jeff Wheeler attended a small college and took his training in physical education from an older coach, who was a father image to all the fellows. When Jeff started his first job in a big city high school, he told the boys they could call him "Jeff." He was really one of the fellows. He talked like them and sat around in the locker room after school to have bull sessions with them. He got a big kick out of telling them about his fraternity life in college.

He wasn't too strict about school rules, either. He laughed along with the boys when they called the principal "Sneaky Sam" because he was always showing up when you least expected him.

However, no one was more surprised than Jeff when he was asked to resign at the end of the school year.

Then one of the boys said, "The trouble with you, Jeff, is you don't act like a teacher. And we know you're not one of us guys."

For once, Jeff took an honest look at himself. He realized that he had stepped out of his role as a teacher, and the boys had little respect for him. They wouldn't turn to him for help if they needed it. Sure, it had been fun to joke around with them. But at what a price! He had been too unprofessional all the way. He resolved to change his ways on the next job.

There are other pitfalls. You might have poor rapport with the parents of your students. You might make too much of an issue over having respect shown to you by making your pupils say meaningless apologies or other hollow phrases. You might scold your students instead of using a little humor to relieve tension.

However, if you realize that you must stay in your role as a teacher to be effective as a mentor of young people, you will be safe. The high ethics of the teaching profession provide guidelines to the beginner as well as the established teacher. But it will be up to you to set the example which you want your students to emulate.

IX

So You Want to Teach in College?

If you are near the top of your class in ability and scholarship and are interested in a career in education, you should consider teaching in a college or university.

There has never been a time when college professors were in such great demand. Nor is it likely that conditions will change in the foreseeable future. In fact, the Carnegie Foundation for the Advancement of Teaching predicts that the nation's colleges will need at least 35,000 more teachers in the seventies than will be available.

The admission officer of a large university in New England declared, "We get ten applications for every student that we can accept. It is heartbreaking to turn away so many eligible young people. But we cannot find enough instructors for them."

The president of a college in the Southwest said recently, "Each year we need more of everything. More buildings. More money. More professors. And it is far easier to expand our plant and raise money than it is to find qualified teachers."

"There aren't enough Ph.D. candidates to go around," complained the personnel director of a women's college in the South. "That's our pool of college teachers. Less than half of them go into teaching nowadays."

109

In the last fifteen years college enrollment has more than doubled. It soared from 2.2 million to about 5.4 million in the 2,200 institutions of higher learning in the United States. Of course, this rapid increase in the number of undergraduate students has taxed the faculty, although nearly 200,000 people are members of instructional staffs.

There are other factors that contribute to the shortage of college teachers, too. For one thing, the role of the institutions of higher learning has changed in the last few years. Not only are the colleges and universities expected to educate the young people of the nation, but all of the problems of our complex society are dumped on their doorsteps. Government and industry alike turn to the colleges for expert help. How to win the race in space, how to wipe out disease, and how to increase production in a factory are only a few of the requests for advice. As the professors take on more and more research to find solutions to these problems, they have less time for the classroom.

The need for professors now and in the future is very real. Perhaps it would be the right goal for you. However, no one should consider this high echelon of the teaching profession unless he has the intelligence and drive to successfully complete graduate work. Most colleges demand that their professors have a doctorate.

In order to work toward a doctorate degree you must apply for admission to a graduate school of a university. Of course, you must first have your bachelor's degree. The faculty committee will review your application and give careful consideration to your undergraduate scholastic record. You cannot apply unless you have obtained a certain grade point average, and if the graduate school has many applicants, the committee is likely to choose the candidates with the best grades.

Some graduate students work toward a master's degree, which takes from one to two years, depending on the school. With the M.A. out of the way, they then go on for their Ph.D. Others skip the master's and concentrate on the Ph.D. right from the start.

Assuming that you are accepted by a graduate school of your choice as a candidate for a doctor of philosophy degree, you will be assigned to a professor in your special field. He will act as your advisor. Usually two other professors are appointed to act with him as your committee.

Each graduate school has its own requirements which have to be satisfactorily fulfilled before a Ph.D. degree can can be granted. Many schools require a mastery of two foreign languages. There are certain graduate courses which have to be taken; you will have to fulfill these requirements. As a candidate you will also choose a research problem with the approval of your committee. It must be an original piece of work on a problem which has never been explored before. You will spend long hours of research on this problem. In due time you will have to pass a series of oral examinations. In some universities the "orals" are given by a panel of professors. The oral examination covers the whole field in which you are studying. For example, if you are trying to get a Ph.D. in English literature the oral examination could include questions on Shakespeare, Chaucer, Milton, obscure poets of the seventeenth and eighteenth centuries, as well as modern literature.

After passing your "orals" you are then expected to finish your research and write your dissertation. Very often at this point, candidates take positions as instructors in colleges and universities and finish their research and dissertation as they are able.

The dissertation is a learned, carefully done piece of work

which reports the findings and conclusions drawn from the research on the problem. Preparing a dissertation is equivalent to writing an authoritative book on the subject. The dissertation must meet certain rigid standards and be approved by your advisory committee.

Frequently the committee will return the dissertation to the candidate and request certain revisions or more research on some point. When the dissertation is finally accepted and published, it will be placed in the university library and be used as reference material. One of the criteria used to rate a university is the kind of research done and the dissertations written by the Ph.D. candidates. This vast amount of original research is an important reservoir of world knowledge.

From the time a candidate begins working toward a Ph.D. until he actually is granted the degree, a period of eight years has passed, on the average. Although this amount of effort may seem overwhelming when you hear about it, the candidate is experiencing one of the most interesting, stimulating periods of his life.

Candidates majoring in education will be granted a doctor of education rather than a doctor of philosophy degree. Except for foreign languages, which are not included, the requirements for a doctorate in education are the same as those for a Ph.D.

A university professor is not required to have teacher training courses. He is chosen because of his knowledge and training in a given field. Usually he obtains his first position through the recommendation of his graduate advisor. After that he gets offers from other colleges because of his reputation and contacts. Colleges and universities who need additional faculty members contact graduate schools all over the nation for the best possible employees.

National Education Association — Joe Di Dio

The modern teacher helps each child develop a sense of inquiry. Research has proved the essence of learning is discovery.

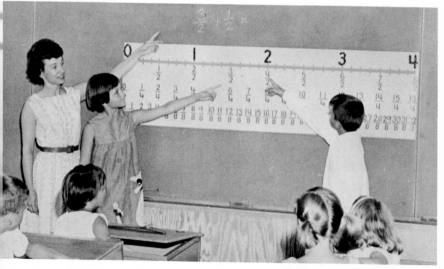

San Juan Unified School District

A third grade teacher is helping her pupils learn about the ruler.

Primary grade pupils learn how to relate their arithmetic lessons to what they will do in their everyday lives.

San Juan Unified School District

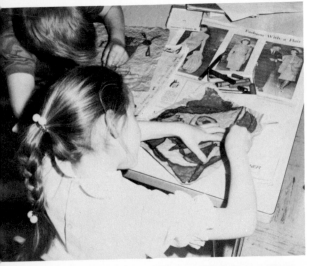

Pupils have art lessons at all grade levels. Special courses prepare the teacher for art instruction.

San Juan Unified School District

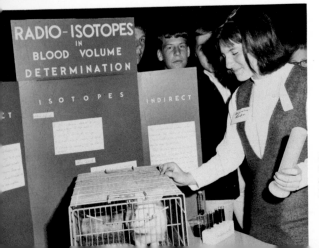

Students are encouraged by their teachers to enter exhibits in science fairs. Such projects stimulate interest in learning science.

San Juan Unified School District

Modern high schools provide extensive laboratory facilities for science classes.

American Seating Company

Instructor and student using a new microscope which enables them to simultaneously view a specimen.

Bausch & Lomb

This instructor and his students built a mock rocket launching control station that actually worked.

San Juan Unified School District

The high school principal wor[ks] closely with the student-body [of]ficers to have varied extra-c[ur]ricular activities.

San Juan Unified School Distr[ict]

The custodian, the teacher a[nd] the principal are importa[nt] members of the school staff. [A] tree planting ceremony is one [of] the many occasions in whi[ch] they work closely together.

San Juan Unified School Distr[ict]

An intern teacher leads the d[is]cussion in a geometry class wh[ile] her supervisor observes. Intern[]ing is a new approach to teach[er] training.

American Seating Compa[ny]

IN THIS TEMPLE
AS IN THE HEARTS OF THE PEOPLE
FOR WHOM HE SAVED THE UNION
THE MEMORY OF ABRAHAM LINCOLN
IS ENSHRINED FOREVER

National Education Association — Carl Purcell
Field trips are an important part of the school curriculum. Thousands of students visit national shrines under the supervision of their teachers.

The principal can help the beginning teacher get off to a successful start.

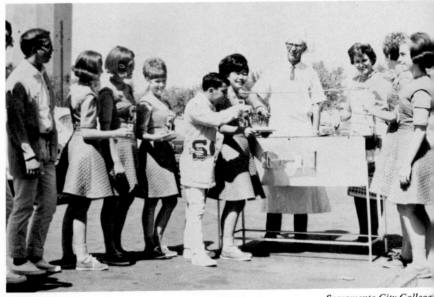

Faculty members are expected to sponsor student activities. Most teachers enjoy this part of their professional duties.

Dramatic art teachers are always in demand on both the high school and college level. It takes expert direction to produce a school play.
San Juan Unified School District

More and more young people are interested in music. Here a choral group is practicing for a school concert.
San Juan Unified School District

The increasing desire to master a musical instrument creates a need for more and more qualified music teachers.
San Juan Unified School District

The swimming instructor does much to prepare young people for a lifetime of participation in water sports.

Football is such a favorite sport that it often has an over-supply of coaches. The young man considering football should have training in other areas as well.

Wrestling is a sport which must be closely supervised by the physical education instructor.

It is the machine shop instructor's responsibility to train boys in a vocation so they can earn a living as adults.

San Juan Unified School District

This business instructor has helped hundreds of young people train for a worthwhile career in office work.

San Juan Unified School District

Ceramics is one of the most popular adult education courses in the United States.
San Juan Unified School District

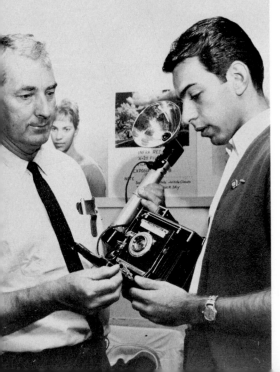

Skilled teachers are needed for such specialized subjects as photography. This junior college instructor gives professional training to a student who hopes to work for a newspaper.
Sacramento City College

Police science is taught in many colleges and universities. Here an instructor explains how automobile accidents occur to these future law enforcement officers.
Sacramento City College

Homemaking teachers are needed for junior and senior high schools.
San Juan Unified School District

Listening carrels are used for many courses in modern secondary schools. Foreign language, public speaking and speech correction are only a few of the classes that make use of this new equipment.
American Seating Company

A teacher supervises a student using a teaching machine. Such machines are excellent when used in drill work and individualized study.

The experienced teacher will have many opportunities to teach in foreign lands. Thousands of teachers take part in exchange programs.

Sacramento City College
The ability to take fingerprints is one of the skills needed by law enforcement officers.

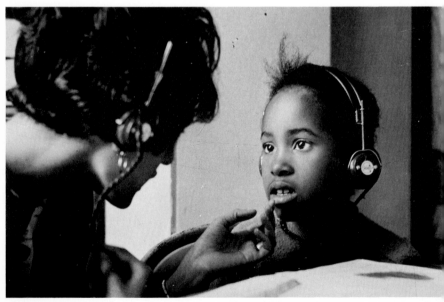

National Education Association — Carl Purcell
Usually a deaf child has a normal speech mechanism, but he cannot use it without training. There is a great need for teachers of handicapped children.

Sacramento City College

The position of school librarian offers all of the advantages of teaching plus interesting duties in pleasant surroundings.

San Juan Unified School District

Both the school superintendent and the principal share the pride of a high school graduate. Strong leadership can help student and teacher to reach their highest aims.

San Juan Unified School District

These three beauty queens who represented their states in a recent Miss America contest are all teachers by profession.

There are three types of higher institutions of learning. These are the university, the college, and the community or junior college.

A university is an institution of learning with one or more undergraduate and graduate schools. A typical university could comprise a school of education, a school of engineering, a school of humanities and sciences, a school of law and a school of medicine, all offering graduate and undergraduate courses.

However, a university might have a graduate school, such as one for divinity students, without an undergraduate school in the field. Some institutions have only graduate schools in the fields of education, law and medicine.

A true university covers many fields of learning or "disciplines" for both undergraduate and graduate students and grants degrees from the bachelor's through the doctorate.

As human problems and world situations have grown more difficult and complex, the universities have had to assume the role of highest authority. These institutions have become one of our great national resources.

The president of the University of California, Clark Kerr, said, "The university has become a prime instrument of national purpose."

The federal government alone spends $15 billion annually on research, most of which is done in the universities. About 70,000 professors (nearly one third of the total) devote their full time to research and do no classroom teaching.

The college also has a valuable place in our educational system. Many colleges have both undergraduate and graduate courses. A college differs from a university in that it does not attempt to cover all the disciplines or fields of learning. A college might have only two schools, one in liberal arts and one in engineering, for example. Generally speaking, a college is thought of as being an institution which provides courses in arts and sciences leading to the bachelor's degree.

A college may have an enrollment as large as a university. The professor in a college might well carry on research and do as much publishing as a professor in a university. However, the emphasis is on the undergraduate work, and the professors usually have regular teaching duties to perform rather than a research assignment.

"Our job is to pass on heritage rather than push out frontiers," a professor of a fine private college said recently.

The third type of higher institution is the community or junior college. The junior college offers the first two years of college or lower division work. Nearly one third of the nation's institutions of higher learning are junior colleges. The U.S. Office of Education reports that one fourth of all college students are now in junior colleges. It estimates that by 1975 one out of two students will attend a two-year college.

Some junior colleges are outposts of universities and are supported by them. They are often called branches or extension centers. Some junior colleges are private institutions, although most of them are part of the local taxing district.

The junior colleges fulfill a major educational need. As the enrollment in the degree-granting institutions soars, more students turn to their community college for their first two years of work. Technical or semiprofessional courses also are offered to those young people wanting job training.

The junior college differs from the other schools in that it usually requires its teachers to have a secondary teaching credential. The majority of instructors in the two-year college have their master's degree. A few hold a doctorate.

Whether you will find your niche in a university, college

or junior college will depend on your achievement, inclination and the opportunity which might present itself at the needed time.

As you prepare for your life as a college teacher you will have to choose a field in which you can become intensely interested. Because of the knowledge explosion it will be impossible for you to become an authority in more than a small phase of your field.

"You have to know more and more about less and less," a physics professor remarked recently. "In science alone there are over fifty thousand journals published each year, to say nothing of all the books and research monographs."

Once you have completed your graduate work and are appointed to a college faculty you will no doubt start out as an instructor. As promotions come you will become an assistant professor, then an associate professor, and finally a full professor.

Typical salaries would be:

Professors	$15,000–20,000
Associate professors	12,000–17,000
Assistant professors	9,000–11,000
Instructors	6,000– 8,000

Of course, the trend is toward higher salaries. Professors who are well-known experts earn much more. Many supplement their salary by acting as consultants to industries and government and by writing textbooks.

More girls who have high scholastic records should aim for the college level of teaching. At the present time over 80 percent of the professors are men.

Another choice you must make is whether to teach in a private or public institution. Where you want to live may influence your choice. Most of the private colleges are in the northeastern states, while the public institutions predominate in the West.

The private, liberal arts college plays an important role in educating young people. Many students succeed better in a college that has small classes with more personalized instruction. Usually the enrollment is less than one thousand. Frequently such colleges are affiliated with a church and offer religious courses.

Only about 25 percent of the faculty members of private, liberal arts colleges hold a Ph.D. degree, and the percentage may drop as the need for college teachers becomes more acute. The young person beginning a teaching career on a college level might be very happy in a private college. More than one half of our colleges are private institutions, but their combined enrollment is one third of the total number of college students. It has been estimated that by 1975 only one fourth of the college students will go to private institutions. The greatest growth is in the public institutions in metropolitan areas.

College life is demanding. Like the housewife's, the professor's work is never done, and he has little leisure time. Although he is not required to spend eight hours in an office and he usually makes out his own schedule, a professor finds that his days are full.

The average professor teaches from twelve to fifteen hours per week. For each hour in the classroom he must allow two hours for preparation. He must also hold office hours so his students can confer with him. He must devote some time to committee and staff meetings. There are graduate students to supervise. Somehow he must find time for research and writing.

However, the life of a college professor has many satisfactions and rewards. He spends his life in an intellectually stimulating atmosphere, his work is purposeful and worthwhile, and his surroundings on a college campus are attractive.

Not only does a professor keep in touch with discoveries in his own field, but he is constantly exposed to new ideas by other members of the faculty. You would seldom be bored on a college campus. As a university president told his staff, "You are on the cutting edge of knowledge."

The majority of college teachers enjoy giving lectures on a subject they know and in which they are intensely interested. Students are in college to learn, and professors find it worthwhile and gratifying to open new horizons to them.

In fact, to bring new insight to bright young minds is an exciting experience. "All of a sudden the sparks fly!" a history teacher explains. "When I really put over a point, the very room bursts into life. My students see it! It's as if I'd opened a door for them!"

A college teacher spends his life around optimistic and enthusiastic young people with boundless hopes for the future, so he, too, tends to stay young in spirit and outlook. Aristotle said a long time ago, "Youth have exalted notions because they have not yet been humbled by life or learned its necessary limitations."

A college professor has an opportunity to influence young people in their thinking, in forming their ideals and frequently in choosing their future vocations.

College students go on to become leaders in their community or even in the nation. A political science professor said, "In a small way, through my students, I'm helping to shape the future of our country. This is a privilege, but almost an overwhelming responsibility, too."

A professor takes satisfaction in the fact that his strength and efforts are used to help students pursue their goals and prepare for their future. William James put it succinctly, "The great use of a life is to spend it on something that will outlast it."

X

Maybe You're Special

Helen Keller, who gained world fame and distinction by overcoming her blindness, deafness and muteness, wrote of her teacher, "I think of Teacher as a spirit giving out warmth, a sun of life." There are thousands of teachers across the nation who are also "giving out warmth." These are the teachers of the exceptional children in the public schools.

An exceptional child is one who deviates intellectually, physically, emotionally or socially from the normal to such an extent that he cannot fully benefit from a regular school program and thus requires special instruction. These include the gifted, mentally and emotionally handicapped, partially sighted and blind, those with impaired hearing or speech defects and the physically handicapped.

The gifted child has an IQ between 130 and 180, or above. Special instruction is needed for these highly intelligent pupils if they are to reach their potential. For many years, these superior children were neglected, and little was done to make the most of this valuable intellectual resource. Then research revealed that far too many of them were under-achievers. One aspect in the revolution taking place in the schools is that of providing for the gifted.

The new educational trends toward nongrading, flexible scheduling and individualized learning do much to meet the needs of the able learner. Some districts provide special classes or schools for the gifted. Many school systems have an accelerated program whereby the gifted pupils can cover three grades of intermediate elementary work or junior high school during two years. It is assumed that the pupil will use the year gained at the graduate level of college for professional training.

Special courses for the more-able learner are offered in junior and senior high schools. Gifted pupils in high schools located near colleges and universities take additional special courses in the higher institutions for which they receive college credit.

Teachers of the gifted should have special attributes. One principal summed up these needs by stating, "Teachers of intellectual pupils should be knowledgeable themselves and have superior skill in at least one field. They should be creative in thought, in teaching and classroom organization. Certainly they should be well organized to advance the aspects of giftedness. It is necessary for the teachers to instill a love of learning, to be flexible in planning lessons and experiences and to be resourceful in searching for special materials." The gifted must be inspired to make the most of themselves so they can make a valuable contribution to society.

There was a time when handicapped children were kept at home and isolated from others. Parents thought they were protecting them. Most people had the attitude, "Why waste money trying to educate children who can never accomplish very much?" But during World War I and World War II, training programs to rehabilitate the war-injured demonstrated that much could be done for the handicapped. Now society expects the public schools to educate the exceptional as well as the normal child. Over 1.5 million pupils are enrolled in special education programs.

"We need exceptional teachers for our exceptional children," a district superintendent said. "Besides being skillful teachers, they must have unusual patience and compassion."

An exceptional child often has a combination of handicaps. Bobby Saunders was such a child. He was mentally retarded, hard of hearing, and had a speech defect. He was teased and ridiculed by the other children in his neighborhood. No matter how hard Bobby tried, he couldn't compete with other youngsters. To him the world was a harsh, unfriendly place.

When Bobby started to school he was placed in a special education class. Here he made friends and found that he could do as well as the other youngsters. His teacher set about to offset all the negative influences in his life. She encouraged him and helped him develop a positive outlook. She worked with him on his speech and hearing problems. She showed him how to make the most of the abilities that he had and become as self-sufficient as possible. Now Bobby is a happy, well-adjusted child.

A teacher who devotes her whole career to handicapped children frequently does so out of a desire to serve humanity. He or she is truly a special person. You, too, might be such a person, and someday find great satisfaction in working with these children.

The mentally retarded make up one of the largest groups of exceptional children. A child whose IQ score falls below 80 is usually considered mentally handicapped. A retarded child can come from any walk of life, but the majority are from the lower socioeconomic, cultural group in the community. Mentally retarded children are often somewhat smaller in stature and are more apt to have physical defects than normal boys and girls. They are often slower in learning to walk and talk.

Basically, however, mentally retarded children have the same needs as any child. They need to feel secure, to be loved and to feel they are valuable, contributing members of a group. They must have purposeful, worthwhile learning experiences. Above all, they need attention.

It is extremely difficult for most of the mentally retarded to satisfy these needs in a normal classroom. Even if they receive individual instruction, they compare themselves with normal children and feel inferior and inadequate. Because such a child is frustrated and cannot get legitimate approval from his classmates, he will often misbehave to gain attention. There are always those who will laugh at his antics and urge him on to defy the teacher. However, when a mentally handicapped youngster is placed in a special class with others like him, where the instruction is geared to his ability, he will generally lose his feelings of inadequacy and will show more self-control in behavior.

"We have three specific objectives in our program," the principal of a special education school said. "These are personal or emotional adjustment, social adjustment, and economic adjustment."

He went on to explain, "We want our boys and girls to be happy and to feel that they have a place in the world. We want them to be able to get along with their parents, their brothers and sisters, and their neighbors. We hope to train the able ones to hold a job. In any case, they should learn to take care of themselves as much as possible."

There are several degrees of retardation, but for special education purposes such mentally handicapped pupils are divided into two groups—the educable and the trainable. Each group has its own special classes and teachers.

A class of educable youngsters includes those whose IQ's fall between 55 and 80. These boys and girls can be taught many subjects such as reading, writing, arithmetic, social studies, language, P.E., art and music. However, the pace is much slower than in the normal classroom. The classes are smaller, generally limited to fifteen or less. Each child receives a great deal of individual help. Since the attention span of mentally handicapped children is limited, the teacher changes the activity frequently.

Older special education pupils in the educable classes receive vocational training. Frequently the high school student works part of the day to get on-the-job experience.

Gary Johnson, an older retarded pupil, was in a work experience program. He went to school in the morning and learned to use tools, to read job instructions and to do arithmetic in relation to construction work. In the afternoon he was an apprentice in a box factory. He became so skilled at his job that he was hired as a full-time employee when he completed his schooling. Like many other mentally retarded people he was trained to be a useful, self-supporting citizen.

When a mentally retarded child has an IQ of less than 55 he is considered trainable although not able to learn minimum academic subjects. He attends a special class for such pupils.

Peggy Littleton, a beautiful little ten-year-old, is in the trainable category with an IQ score of only 45. However, Peggy is very willing to come to school. A small bus picks her up at home each day and takes her to school so she doesn't have to cross busy streets. She loves her teacher, Mrs. Blake. Since there are only twelve children in the class,

Mrs. Blake has time to help her. Peggy is working very hard to learn to speak more clearly.

The children especially enjoy music. Many times during the day, they gather around the piano and sing while Mrs. Blake plays. Peggy often plays the tambourine while they sing. All of the pupils participate in a rhythm band.

There are lots of puzzles, games and art supplies available so there is something interesting to do all the time. Peggy has learned to paint, to color, to put jigsaw puzzles together and to string beads. She has learned to tie her shoelaces, take off her rain boots and coat, and keep track of her belongings.

Many times during the day, the boys and girls go out on the playground. They learn to play ball, jump rope and ride tricycles, which help to develop their coordination. Peggy and the other children learn to get along with other people. Peggy has conquered her shyness and fear of being in a strange place. She has attained good health habits, also, such as keeping her face and hands clean and her hair combed. She can take herself to the lavatory.

Peggy, like others in her class, will always have to be supported. No doubt, she will spend much of her life in an institution. But the training Peggy receives in her special class will help her all of her life. She has founds ways to occupy her time happily, and is better able to communicate with others and take care of her physical needs. Although it is costly to train Peggy in school, a great deal of money will be saved in the long run. Because she has become more self-sufficient, she will require much less care at home or in an institution.

Some children are emotionally disturbed or neurologically handicapped due to brain damage, cerebral palsy or other psychogenic conditions. A large school system will have special classes for these children. Their teacher will work under the direction of a psychiatrist. Sometimes these children are placed in the special education classes with the mentally retarded.

Usually a committee consisting of the school psychologist, doctor, social worker, school nurse and principal of receiving school will review the case history of a child before he is placed in a special education class. The parents are consulted, too. The main question in everyone's mind is, "Will placement in a special class be in the best interest of this child?"

A low IQ or a neurological condition is not the only factor considered. A child's social and emotional adjustment is given close attention. Some retarded children function adequately in a normal classroom with special instruction. A child is placed in a special class when he cannot gain from the regular school program.

The key person in the special education program is the teacher. Mentally handicapped children need a great deal of direction and understanding. The teacher should have a warm and friendly personality and be able to accept retarded children for what they are. Of course, she should be genuinely interested in their welfare.

To obtain a credential for teaching the mentally handicapped the candidate is usually required to take part of her practice teaching with a normal class and complete it with a special class. A teacher must have experience with normal children before she can understand those who deviate. Her training includes courses in child growth and development, abnormal psychology, speech therapy, as well as methods for teaching the mentally handicapped. She will also have training in crafts, physical education and music.

Children with impaired vision make up another group of exceptional boys and girls. This group is divided into the partially sighted and the blind. The partially sighted child is considered as one who sees and can use his sight to help him learn although his vision is between 20/70 and 20/200 with correction. The blind pupil has less than 20/200 vision with correction.

There are several plans in use to provide schooling for the partially sighted and blind children. Some attend public or private residential schools. However, the trend is toward keeping the child at home. A city system may have a special school or rooms where all of the youngsters with impaired vision are brought together.

If possible the child is kept in a regular school. Some schools then have a cooperative plan in which youngsters do work requiring close use of their eyes in a special room but share all of the other activities with their classmates. Also a commonly used arrangement is where there is a resource room with a special teacher. The pupil does his work with his class and goes to the resource room for materials and training at designated times.

Finally, there is the itinerant teacher plan. The student is registered in the regular grade and does all of his work there. The itinerant teacher comes to him with special materials and trains him in their use. She also acts as a counselor and helps him learn to cope with his problems.

The school system provides special equipment for the partially sighted pupil, such as magnifiers, tape recorders, Dictaphones and typewriters. Large type books, wide-lined paper, and pencils with thick dark lead which does not smear and quaver also help the child in his studies.

Most partially sighted children learn to use typewriters

when they are in the fourth grade. Some are ready when they are in the third grade.

Kindergarten has special significance for the partially sighted child, for it is here he gets oriented to the classroom, the school building and the playground.

Teachers of partially sighted pupils have learned to slow the pace of their lessons. As one explained, "It takes these children longer to focus their eyes so they can gain a clear image. We can't be in too much of a hurry."

If you observe a special teacher working with these children, you will notice that she trains them to listen carefully. She might say, "Go to the easel and find two paintbrushes. Then bring them to me." If the child brings only one paintbrush, she explains the importance of listening to directions. She will try another child, "Go to the toy box and find the big ball."

To teach the children spatial relations she might say, "You have a large piece of newsprint. Can you draw a line down the left side of it? Good. Now make a circle in each corner."

Some partially sighted children have poor coordination, so they are urged to skip, hop and throw bean bags to develop this skill.

The primary aim of education for the partially sighted is to develop a well-adjusted child who can live as normally as possible and have a chance to be self-supporting as an adult.

The child who is completely blind presents still different challenges to the teacher. Such a youngster must be taught to function independently. He must learn to use his other physical, mental and emotional endowments to the fullest degree. Here, too, the educational goal is to help him adjust to his problem and get the maximum benefit from his schooling.

Blind students must develop their ability to listen and to analyze what they hear. They must remember what they have learned from previous lessons.

Boys and girls who are sightless learn to read and write in braille. This system is named after Louis Braille, a blind Frenchman, who developed it in 1829 when he was only twenty years old to aid him in teaching other blind people. Braille is based on a series of cells with embossed dots which are arranged two wide and three high. A cell could be any one of sixty-three possible combinations of dots. The braille code has 185 contractions, which simplify reading and writing. A child memorizes the various combinations of embossed dots. He reads by running his fingertips over the raised cells.

The blind youngster learns to write on a braillewriter. He also uses a braille slate which is light enough to carry. He memorizes braille codes for music and mathematics. In order to have written communication with the sighted, he learns to use a typewriter. He also finds out how to use the various electronic devices to help detect obstacles and steps while walking. The teacher has the responsibility of helping the blind pupil learn to operate this equipment skillfully and rapidly without becoming discouraged and overtired.

The teacher helps blind children live in a sighted world. For example, these boys and girls learn to eat properly and to groom themselves with the least assistance. They soon are able to find their way around in the schoolroom and on the playground. They learn recreational activities so they can enjoy their leisure time.

Another group of exceptional children who need special instruction are those with permanently impaired hearing. The handicap of deafness affects all of a child's forms of communication: understanding, speaking, reading, writing, as well as hearing. The most noticeable result of deafness is poor speech. Although a deaf child nearly always has a normal speech mechanism, he cannot use it correctly without training because he does not hear himself.

Communication is a two-way process. A child should understand what is said to him and be able to express his thoughts. Communication with others is one of the most important factors in the development of a child's personality and in his learning.

Children with impaired hearing fall into many different categories, each of which presents different problems. Some children have been deaf since birth, which makes it very difficult for them to learn to speak. Others have lost their hearing after they have established their speech patterns, but it is necessary for them to maintain their ability to talk. Hearing loss often produces psychological stresses which must be considered.

A machine called an audiometer is used to measure hearing ability in terms of decibels, which indicate the intensity of sound. For example, a faint whisper is about 15 decibels, average speech is 60 decibels, and a siren some distance away might register 140 decibels. Children who show a mild, marginal or moderate loss are classified as hard of hearing. Those who have severe or profound loss are considered deaf.

Researchers have uncovered many facts about hearing. For example, most people hear better in the left ear than in the right. More boys than girls have defective hearing. When a child is about twelve years old his hearing reaches its maximum and then declines slowly as he grows older. Vowels which are low in pitch are understood more easily than consonants which are high.

Hearing therapists or special teachers use audio equipment, with earphones for each child, to amplify the sound so all except the totally deaf can hear. By using this equipment many lessons are taught. Of course, speech improvement is an important part of the curriculum. The teacher gets samples of each pupil's speech on a tape recorder. She evaluates the articulation, quality, pitch and melody. The children listen to their own voices through the audio equipment. Then the teacher helps them develop new neuromuscular patterns to produce better speech.

The hard-of-hearing and deaf children are also taught lipreading. "They soon learn to use facial expressions, gestures and situational clues to interpret what has been said," a speech therapist explained.

After the pupils learn the basic principles of lipreading, the teacher introduces distracting sounds in the background which the children must learn to ignore. Finally they are taken on excursions and are expected to lip-read under many different situations.

Auditory training, which improves a child's listening skill, is an important part of the curriculum. A youngster learns to discriminate between the various noises in his environment; he becomes aware of the rhythm patterns of music and speech; and he seeks out the difficult consonant sounds when someone is speaking to him.

It is important for the deaf child to learn to read as soon as possible. Special teachers of the deaf have found that the more the child knows about language—sentence structure, use of an extensive vocabulary, ability to spell, along with reading—the better he is able to function in spite of his handicap.

There are children who have speech handicaps who are not hard of hearing or deaf. A child might stutter or stammer or speak in a jargon. He might be delayed in speech development or have a voice defect.

Some speech problems are the result of physical conditions such as cleft palate, cerebral palsy or brain injury. Aphasia is loss of speech due to brain injury. Other speech problems come from a child's emotional difficulties.

Many school systems have speech correctionists on their staff. Sometimes these specialists are called speech therapists or speech teachers. Each correctionist is assigned a certain number of schools where she works with the classroom teacher to identify the children with incorrect speech. The therapist then works out a weekly schedule to help as many children as possible.

A speech correctionist usually has had a drama or speech major in college. In addition to the general education and psychology courses required for a teacher's certificate, the correctionist has had extensive training in phonetics, anatomy and physiology of the speech mechanism. This specialist has learned to recognize and classify speech problems. Courses in therapy and supervised clinical practice are also part of the correctionist's background.

The physically handicapped are another group among exceptional children. Nearly all school districts have pupils with various crippling conditions who need to be educated. Some children have congenital defects such as missing limbs; a clubfoot; Erb's palsy, which paralyzes the muscles of the shoulder, arm and hand; or the complex neuromuscular disability called cerebral palsy. Other children have postural defects or deformities. Still others have epilepsy, cardiac conditions or metabolic disturbances or any one of the hundreds of disabilities that affect children.

If possible, the physically handicapped child is integrated

in the regular classroom. However, a large district usually finds it necessary to set aside special rooms or even an entire building for the exceptional children who are too disabled to attend other schools. A special classroom for the disabled is designed to accommodate those in wheelchairs as well as those on crutches or wearing braces. There are ramps instead of steps, wide doors and tables of special heights.

Appropriate lavatory facilities are adjacent to the room. There is often an anteroom with cots for those who must have rest periods. Close by is an enclosed playground with special equipment for suitable physical activity.

The classes are small so each pupil has a maximum of individual help. Besides the special teachers, the school personnel usually include a physical therapist and a full-time nurse.

"An education means everything to the crippled child!" a teacher in a special school said. "Even if he never leaves his wheelchair he can explore the whole world through his mind."

Another teacher added, "We are laying the foundation for vocational training, too. Besides, he mustn't spend his leisure time just waiting. We help him learn to do creative things in art, music or hobbies. These will carry over to enrich his adulthood."

Many school systems provide special schooling for children and young people who are confined to their homes. These pupils may be recuperating from accidents, illnesses or operations, and are housebound temporarily. Others may have a physical or an emotional disability which makes it impossible for them to leave home. The home teacher generally spends an hour a week with each pupil. This special teacher brings textbooks, workbooks and other material and assigns lessons for one week. She also answers questions and

collects the completed lessons from the previous week. There
are home teachers for both the elementary and secondary
levels.

The culturally deprived child presents another problem to
the school. Children from very poor homes who have had
limited background and few opportunities for outside experiences are handicapped in a special way. Sometimes these
pupils are unable to speak English, and frequently they need
remedial reading.

Compensatory education is a new development which at-
tempts to bring the deprived child up to a cultural level
where he can gain the most from school and compete with
his more fortunate classmates. The field of compensatory
education also offers openings to special teachers.

Although you must have special training to teach exceptional children, there are advantages in this field. There is
always a great demand for special teachers. Classes are
smaller and in many areas the salary is larger. Of course, you
must be interested in working with exceptional children.
Many teachers prefer a normal class, but the teacher of exceptional children has the reward of knowing that she is
truly helping those who desperately need her.

XI

You Don't Have to Teach

So you want to be where the action is—but you don't want to teach! Then consider one of the many other careers in education.

Perhaps you will agree with Becky Lewis, the teen-age daughter of a biology professor in a private college. Her mother also taught, in a high school in the college town. Becky's parents took it for granted that she, too, would become a teacher. But Becky had misgivings.

One afternoon after school, while she waited in the college library for her father, she confided in Mrs. Calland, the head librarian and a family friend.

"Golly, Mrs. Calland, I don't know what to do. You know how my folks feel about my becoming a teacher."

"Yes, I know."

"Of course, science is my best subject in high school. But I just can't get excited about teaching it. I guess with both Mom and Dad teaching I'm too close to it."

"What about being a research technician?" Mrs. Calland asked.

"That leaves me cold, too. I've been around laboratories all of my life! I've fed Daddy's white rats since I could walk!" Becky answered. She managed a small smile. "See how mixed up I am?"

Mrs. Calland had a thoughtful expression on her face. Then she said, "Becky, have you ever considered becoming a science librarian? You could major in science in college and then take a graduate year in library training. A science librarian could get a position in any number of universities. With your background, you'd be perfect for such a job!"

A wide smile lighted Becky's face. "Mrs. Calland, that's a terrific idea! I think I'd like that! You know how I love to read. How I'm always hanging around here. I'll talk to Mom and Dad about it tonight."

"Point out to them that you would have all the advantages of teaching, Becky. Of course, I think being a librarian is the best possible career."

Never has there been such a demand for school librarians on all levels, from elementary through university. The shortage of trained personnel for school libraries becomes more acute each year. About thirty thousand librarians are employed in the schools.

If you really enjoy books and reading, if you like to be around people and serve them, if you want a variety of activities in pleasant surroundings, you should consider becoming a school librarian. You would be classified as a regular member of the staff with the same salary schedule, tenure, retirement benefits and sick leave as the teachers. This career is open to men and women of all ethnic groups.

In college, you will no doubt be advised to take a liberal arts course that includes social sciences, sociology, psychology and literature. If possible you should work in a library as a student assistant. Your graduate year will be spent in one of more than thirty approved library schools. Upon completion of this training you will be granted an M.A. degree.

As the school librarian you would select and order the required reference materials that the faculty and students need. These materials include books, periodicals, filmstrips, records, films, maps, newspapers and flat pictures. Your library might be the center for movie projectors, radios, television sets and other electronic equipment used in the school.

You would be responsible for planning and arranging the library quarters, its furnishings and equipment. You would have to be familiar with all the courses of study offered in the school, so you could provide the best reference and enrichment materials for them. You would be the materials specialist. As such, it will be necessary for you to catalog the books and periodicals in relation to the curriculum, as well as according to accepted library standards.

No school library can operate without student help, so it will be up to you to train and supervise these assistants. Also, on the secondary and elementary levels, you no doubt will teach courses in library science and train the pupils to use the card catolog, reference books and the readers' guides. Too, you will help students learn the basics of the Dewey Decimal and the Library of Congress systems of classification. If you are in an elementary school, you will have storytelling sessions to introduce small children to the world of books.

A school librarian ought to have a broad education with some insight into every major phase of human endeavor. You will be asked to find reference materials on every subject ranging from cryogenics to Chinese literature. In addition, you must be a reading expert and be able to match the interest and abilities of the pupils with the books. It is an art in itself to find the high-interest book for the poor reader and the challenging book for the gifted student.

You will need to be a guidance expert, too, for young people will seek answers to their emotional problems in books or look for information on careers and vocations. A school librarian ought to be a good business person and be able to make wise purchases and balance the library budget.

In considering the opportunities for library work, you should also investigate those on the college and university level. You will find that there is always need for special librarians with background and training enabling them to serve in schools of medicine, law, engineering, mineral science and business, to name a few. You might prefer to work in the main college library and eventually be in charge of a room or several rooms or the whole library. The head librarian of a university will earn from $12,000 to $20,000 a year.

To get further information about library schools, employment opportunities and the many available scholarships, write to:

American Library Association
50 East Huron Street
Chicago 11, Illinois

or

Special Library Association
31 East Tenth Street
New York 3, New York

Another nonteaching school staff member is the social worker. This person may be known by other titles such as "child welfare officer" or "visiting teacher." Under whatever name the social worker serves, his or her contribution to the welfare of young people in school and to the total community is most important. The social worker endeavors to improve the relations between parents and school personnel by helping them understand each other. The social worker investigates the pupils' environment and reports on the factors that affect their behavior. Also, the trained social worker can assist the pupil in need of help through the process of referral to the available community resources.

A professional social worker must have six years of college preparation. The undergraduate years are usually devoted to a general course that includes economics, sociology, social anthropology, political science, psychology and statistics. The two following years are spent in an accredited graduate school offering specialized training and supervised field work, leading to a master's degree in social work. At the end of this preparation, the social worker is qualified to be employed by any one of many agencies, including a public school district.

Some states issue a special certificate to social workers desiring school employment. Arizona is one state that has this arrangement. The requirements for a certificate in Arizona include an M.A. in social work and one of the following: (a) one year field instruction in a school system; (b) prior employment in a school system; (c) or six semester hours of course work in organization and philosophy of public schools.

Don Carman has been a school social worker in a large city for five years. He does most of his work with high school boys who are usually, but not always, from the slums.

On a typical day, Don will investigate truancy cases which might stem from the fact that the boys have no suitable clothes to wear or not enough food to eat. Don will also go to juvenile court and to the police department on behalf of pupils who have been arrested. His day might include some casework with a boy whose family life has been disrupted. Another important phase of his work is finding reasons why an able learner gets poor grades.

Don is often asked, "Don't you get depressed working in the slums so much? All you hear about is trouble!"

To that Don answers, "I try to analyze what can be done to help my clients instead of dwelling on what has happened to them. Don't forget that I'm not the only one who deals with students who are in trouble. The principal, the counselors, the school doctors and nurses get their share, too."

For additional information about a career as a school social worker write to:

Council on Social Work Education, Inc.
345 East 46th Street
New York 17, New York

or

National Federation of Settlements, Inc.
226 West 47th Street
New York 36, New York

The school health services offer many career opportunities to those who have received proper training. A large school district might have doctors, nurses, audiometrists, vision technicians, dentists, dental hygienists and therapists on its staff. A dietitian, who works on the school lunch program, would be available as a consultant in nutrition.

Of course, promoting and protecting the health of the students and school personnel is one of the main services of this medical staff. It goes without saying that the better a child's health is, the more able he is to learn.

In many districts the pupils get a medical screening or examination by doctors and nurses before participating in advanced physical education or athletics. Another responsibility of the staff is giving emergency treatment in the case of accidents or sudden illness at school.

The doctors and nurses work tirelessly to control and prevent communicable diseases. Clinics are held to immunize the children. As another means of controlling diseases in most schools, the nurse must readmit the pupil who has been absent due to illness after a certain length of time.

The school doctors check on the water supply and sewage disposal of a school. They investigate the heating, ventilation and lighting in the school. They inspect the lavatories, kitchens, gymnasiums, showers, swimming pools and locker rooms, to make sure that conditions are clean and sanitary. They also supervise the food handlers in the school.

In nearly all states the school nurse must hold a public health license. She assists the doctor in his work. But her most important responsibility is that of health counseling. It is the school nurse who talks with the pupils and their parents about health problems. She explains the recommendations of the doctor and helps the parents and pupils think through to solutions of their problems. Too, the nurse works closely with the teachers in the health education aspects of the curriculum.

In most school districts, the nurse has charge of the weighing and measuring of the pupils. She is likely to be the one who conducts the vision screening test. However, a large district might have a vision technician on its staff.

The nurse might also do the hearing tests. Very often, however, there is a trained audiometrist who measures the hearing of pupils. Those youngsters with hearing loss are referred to ear specialists for treatment.

A few very large districts employ a dentist as a consultant, but most school systems work with a dentist from the health department or dental society. The dentist supervises the dental program in the schools, including the work of the dental hygienists. Many districts have hygienists who inspect the teeth of the pupils and advise the parents when treatment is necessary. The dental hygienist also assists the teachers in dental health instruction.

The program for the physically handicapped usually necessitates having a therapist on the staff. A nurse is usually assigned full time to a school with classes for the physically handicapped.

The psychological services play an essential role in the modern school. Staff members include psychometrists, psychologists and psychiatrists either on a full-time or part-time basis. Often psychiatrists in private practice are called in as consultants.

Individual psychological tests are given to pupils who may be in need of special placement. Such tests help identify pupils who are gifted or retarded, emotionally disturbed or neurologically handicapped. Tests are given to pupils with emotional problems who remain in regular classes.

It takes a skilled person with special training to give an individual psychological test and get valid results. Many phases of the test call for expert interpretation. A psychometrist is a person with this training and is certificated by state authorities to administer these psychological tests. A psychometrist either is employed by the school district or is on the staff of the county superintendent of schools. Sometimes the state department of education hires these trained people. The principal of the local school requests his services when necessary.

The work of the psychometrist is most interesting and offers still another career in education for both men and women. Usually the pay of the psychometrist is equivalent to that of a teacher. To be informed about the training necessary to become a psychometrist you might consider the requirements for the state of Idaho, as an example. A pupil personnel service certificate endorsed for psychological examiner is issued. The applicant must have an acceptable master's degree from an accredited college or university.

In addition, the applicant must have completed the following:

1. Nine hours of psychology—general; human growth and development; and advanced educational psychology.
2. Twelve hours of education in methods or curriculum development and laboratory experience.
3. Six hours of psychological methods—measurement; statistics; individual testing; counseling principles and techniques.
4. Six hours of school organization and program—exceptional child; diagnostic and remedial instruction.
5. Internship of 120 clock hours.

The school psychologist either administers tests himself or uses the results of a test given by a psychometrist to make a diagnosis of a pupil's educational ability and emotional problems. He counsels with parents, children and school personnel and provides expert advice as to a course of action which should be followed. He is consulted in the placement of children in special classes. His services are invaluable in helping the maladjusted child who is hostile, withdrawn, overaggressive or depressed.

A school psychologist must have a master's degree in psychology or education, and he needs thorough training in both fields. It takes at least two graduate years to fulfill the requirements of most states. A long internship or clinical experience is also necessary.

A psychiatrist is a medical doctor. He works either on a full-time basis or as a consultant to supervise the education of the emotionally disturbed or neurologically handicapped pupils in the public schools.

One of the most interesting nonteaching careers in the schools is that of counseling. Many districts use counselors at the elementary level as well as the secondary.

The counselor works with the students to help them understand themselves and adjust to their particular life situation, to assist them in formulating appropriate goals, and to give them information so the pupils can make independent decisions about training for careers or vocations. The counselor works with parents and school personnel in regard to student problems and plans.

The counselor is a liaison between the pupils and community agencies and referral services. The program of testing individual talents and aptitudes is the responsibility of the counselor. Keeping attendance records and organizing the comprehensive cumulative pupil records is an important part of the counselor's work.

Nearly all states require special training for the guidance counselor. The requirements for pupil counseling in the state of California might be considered as an example. They are:

1. Master's degree or higher.
2. Course in pupil personnel services concepts and procedures; dynamics of individual behavior; measurement theory and procedures; counseling theory and procedures; group process measurement and procedure; educational and career planning; remedial and special education; research methodology; laws relating to children; organization of pupil personnel services.
3. Sixty hours of graduate work, or three years of classroom teaching and thirty hours.
4. At least 480 clock hours of supervised field experience.

If you could observe Charles Leedy, a counselor in a large high school on the East Coast, you would see how much he enjoys his work. Every morning the waiting room outside his office is filled with pupils seeking readmittance slips after absence from school. In a short time these slips have been granted, and the boys and girls leave for the first-period class.

Mr. Leedy's first appointment is with Nick Galiopus, a senior. Nick begins, "I came to see if you would know where I could learn to be a chef. My uncle owns a restaurant, and he wants to take me into business with him. But my dad wants me to get some training first."

The counselor answers, "How fortunate you are, Nick! That's an excellent vocation. Naturally, everyone has to eat. I think your father is wise to have you take some training first. You would be more of an asset to your uncle after you had been trained."

"Sure, that's right. And maybe my uncle doesn't know everything about running his business, either."

Mr. Leedy gets up and walks to his filing cabinet. "I have quite a bit of material to show you. I'll loan you whatever you want so you can study it and show it to your father and uncle. There are several places where you can train to be a chef. You might also consider courses in restaurant management as well."

For the next fifteen minutes, Mr. Leedy and Nick examine the many pamphlets and booklets. Nick chooses the most pertinent ones to take home.

Mr. Leedy's next appointment is with Martha Westenburg. When she comes in and sits down, he begins, "I have this note from your mother requesting that you be excused early every Wednesday afternoon to take singing lessons."

"I really need the lessons, Mr. Leedy. I'm going to sing

professionally with a combo. I'm calling myself Marti West."
She laughs a little self-consciously. "Maybe you'll see me on
television someday."

"I hope so, Martha. I've heard you sing at school functions
and you're good. But about these lessons—can't you take
them after school?"

"The music studio doesn't have any time free then."

"But it means that you would miss English literature once
a week. As you know, that's a required course." He picks up
her cumulative record and studies it. "You have only a C
average in that course as it is. What would you do if you
missed one period a week?"

"Well, I don't know. But I just *have* to have those lessons."

"Of course, you want to take the lessons. But do you really
think you can afford to lose school time for them? Are there
any other arrangements you could make?"

"Well, I guess I could take group lessons on Saturday.
There are some openings then."

"Perhaps you would prefer the private lessons, but would
you be willing to try the group lessons for a while? In the
meantime, you could raise your grade in English. Then we'll
discuss this matter later."

"Well, OK, I'll try the group lessons for now. That's what
my folks want me to do, too. But I talked Mom into asking
for time off."

"I think you've made a wise decision, Martha. Come back
soon and tell me about the lessons. They sound great."

All during the day Mr. Leedy helps boys and girls come to
their own decisions regarding their problems. It is his role
to give them as much information as possible and help them
examine all the factors sensibly and objectively. He works
with the parents and tries to avoid interfering with the child-
parent relationship.

Counselors play an important part in keeping students in school. They make every effort to keep pupils from becoming dropouts. Frequently they arrange work-training for the potential dropout so he can work part time and attend school the remainder of the day.

There are many aspects to the counselor-guidance career which make it a most desirable one to consider. The modern school has responsibilities beyond the imparting of knowledge and developing of basic skills. The welfare of the whole individual must be considered, and to help a pupil develop his potentialities to their fullest takes a counseling expert to work with the teachers.

Even if you don't want to teach, do consider all of the other positions in education for a worthwhile career, for security and good pay. Remember, you don't have to teach to be a part of the exciting world of a school.

XII

Your Hand at the Helm

The day started as usual at McKinley High School. School buses pulled up next to the side entrance and unloaded. Students drove shiny new sportscars and stripped-down hot rods into the crowded parking area. The November wind whipped a sheet of paper across the frozen lawn and flattened it against the fence.

Boys and girls streamed into the corridors. Locker doors banged. A warning bell rang. At last all eight hundred students were settled temporarily in their homerooms with their books piled high on the wide arms of their chairs.

The PA system crackled a minute and the familiar voice of the principal began, "Good morning, this is Mr. Peterson. I have an announcement to make, and I must say that I'm speaking with mixed emotions. I regret to tell you that due to ill health, our assistant superintendent, Mr. Alden, has had to resign. This came as a great surprise to all of us. I have been appointed to take his place, effective immediately. A new principal will take over here. In the meantime I know you will all cooperate with the vice-principals."

A new principal! Mr. Peterson had been the principal at McKinley High School ever since it had been built fifteen years ago. It was hard to imagine anyone else in his place. The boys and girls stared at each other in surprise. The

147

teachers commented on how everyone would miss Mr. Peterson. Then each one began to wonder how this change would affect him.

Gary Hall, editor of the school paper, leaned forward and whispered to the girl in front of him, "Man, I hope this new guy keeps off my back. I've got a lot of ideas for new features in the paper. Old Peterson had given his OK. But will the new one?"

Miss Wyatt, at the front of the room, looked at him and frowned. "No talking, Gary." She went on, "I have some announcements to make." But while she spoke, she wondered to herself, A new principal! Would he come in with a lot of new ideas? Stir them all up? Would they have to change their lesson plans? Would he want to try the new methods? Team teaching? Nongraded classes?

In the gymnasium the football coach said to his assistant, "Did you hear that? Maybe the new man won't approve of competitive sports!"

The office clerk groaned to the school nurse, "But we're all so used to Mr. Peterson! And we just reorganized our record system."

The head cook said to her cafeteria helper, "Well, I hope the new principal will get us a walk-in refrigerator. I think I had Mr. Peterson convinced. Now I don't know."

Two custodians were stacking chairs in the storeroom. One said, "Did you hear that we're getting a new principal?"

The other one grumbled, "Well, I hope this one does something about Mrs. Forbes, the art teacher. I do nothin' but run errands for that old gal." He mimicked, " 'Help me unload my kiln! Reach up and get me that ream of art paper! Bring me a new pug of clay!' " He banged a chair on the stack. "Somebody'd better do somethin' about her!"

When the head bus driver heard the news he thought,

Now maybe we can get a new bus! Peterson turned me down.

The president of the P.T.A. called one of her chairman and told her the news. Then she asked, "Do you suppose the new principal will let us hold our Christmas Bazaar?"

A change of principals in any of the approximately 150,000 public and private schools would have a decided effect on it just as it did at McKinley High School.

The work of a principal has many aspects. The principal must be all things to all people. He has to be an educator, business manager and public relations expert all at one time.

There is always need for administrators. Perhaps you have the qualities for leadership which would make this field of education a good one for you.

How should you go about becoming a principal? Of course, you have to obtain your administrator's credential before you can be appointed. Such a credential is required in almost all states.

In Chapter 4 it was pointed out that a teacher's credential and at least two years' teaching experience are usually prerequisites to administrative training. You would attend summer or regular sessions at a college or university offering courses in school administration. These courses cover areas such as school law, testing, pupil personnel services, guidance, evaluating, health services, special education, plant planning and management, curriculum development and personnel selection.

After taking a required number of courses you no doubt will be assigned to a principal for supervised field study to observe and assist him for at least a semester. You can usually arrange to do this while you are teaching.

At last you have your credential and your appointment and are ready to begin as a principal. You will find that you will have a great deal more responsibility than you did as a teacher. Too, you will be on the job long before the school year begins and after it closes. You will have fewer holidays. You will be the first one at school and the last to leave.

The welfare of the boys and girls who attend your school should be uppermost in your mind. After all, the school exists for the students. Your attitude toward them will set the whole tone of the school. Above all, you must understand and have empathy for the young people in your care. You should believe in the worth of young people and be convinced that the vast majority are a credit to their parents and community. The delinquent boy or girl is the exception rather than the rule.

As a good principal, you will remember that each student is entitled to the best possible education appropriate for him. This means that you must identify and provide proper learning experiences for the gifted or more-able learner. You must strive for maximum achievement from the majority of your pupils. You will also need to provide special instruction for the slow learner and the retarded. A great deal of your time will be spent in planning and developing the curriculum to achieve these aims. It will be up to you to decide what new methods as well as what traditional ones will work best for your particular school. You must lead the way toward better practices as you will be director of curriculum.

As a principal you will have to make the final decision as to what school activities would be worthwhile and not a waste of time. Take sports, for example. Should they be intramural or competitive? Who is eligible? How about student government? How do you supervise your student council without dominating it? Should you have a school newspaper? A yearbook? Plays? Programs? How often should you hold assemblies? How do you involve as many students as possible in activities so they aren't just a showcase for the aggressive few.

Your role as counselor will be important. Your advice will be sought by students and parents alike to help solve difficult problems. Over and over you will be asked questions such as, "Would you say that my Dora is emotionally disturbed?" "What's wrong with Eddie? He doesn't want to come to school." "We're getting a divorce. How will it affect our kids?" "I'd like to be a doctor. Do you think I can make it?" "Where should I go to college?" One trait you must develop is the ability to exercise good judgment based upon each specific situation and need.

You will find that it is your job to establish the disciplinary policies of your school. You must make the final decision as to what actions should not be tolerated and what punishment should be meted out.

Your discipline should be constructive and not always just restrictive. Should you expect good citizenship or reward it? Should citizenship be graded? Should good citizenship be a requirement for those participating in school sports and activities? One high school in California issues senior privilege cards which entitle the deserving last-year student to special consideration. For example, he can use the library instead of the study hall. He can sit in an unsupervised section in assemblies. He has a permanent hall pass. You must work out your own positive discipline policies.

Of one thing you can be certain: all the difficult discipline problems will eventually end up in your office. Somehow you must find the skill to handle them. Usually the parents of the offender will be involved before you are through. Often these parents will be angry and on the defensive. And as one junior high principal pointed out, "The parent whose own control has ceased to exist expects the most from us!"

You will find that the problems have changed in the last few years. A vice-principal of a large school in New Mexico reported recently, "We've found that our pupils don't fight as much on the school grounds. And they seem to behave better in the classroom." To that, an administrator in New York might retort, "We've noticed that, too, but the problems are more serious. There's more vandalism. More drinking at school functions. Cheating in examinations. Cutting school. Vulgarity. And downright defiance."

The safety of your pupils will be your concern. It will be your responsibility to keep your school grounds and buildings free from hazards. It will be up to you to prevent accidents by enforcing safety rules. You will need to hold regular fire drills and air raid drills.

Not long ago an elementary school auditorium in the South was packed with youngsters who were watching a puppet show. Pupils from a neighboring school had been bussed over for the event. In the middle of the show, a fire broke out on the stage from defective electric wiring. In an instant flames burst out from the stage curtains. The principal jumped up and directed the evacuation of the room. Because the children had been so carefully trained in fire drills they marched out in orderly rows and lined up in a safe place. There was not one casualty. Later the fire chief said, "I never saw anything like it. They could have panicked and trampled each other to death."

Your relationship with your teachers will be an important phase of your work. Some principals have charge of/or take part in hiring their teachers. You must be skillful in selecting good staff members. In a large school district, however, there is usually a special personnel office that recruits all of the employees.

In any case it is your task to assign your teachers to their position on the staff. It takes a great deal of skill to select the right teacher for the right place, assigning him to the pupils who would gain the most from him. Teachers do not always know where they would function the best, either. Sometimes a teacher is in a primary grade when she should be on the intermediate level. A mediocre music teacher might make a superior English teacher. You might have a junior high teacher who should be in special education. You need to develop a sixth sense to place your staff members properly.

Not only do you assign your teachers but you must supervise their activities. Nearly all of your teachers will need assistance to reach their highest level of performance. The supervisory duties of a principal are now greatly emphasized.

You might have a beginning teacher who will need encouragement and genuine help to get off to a good start. Too many inexperienced teachers are left on their own to flounder around as best they can.

An experienced teacher new to your school and your community will need help in finding resource material and in becoming acquainted with the pupils and their parents. You can help such a person become oriented to the new situation.

You could have an old-timer on the staff who is just plain inefficient and "set in his ways." It may require an indirect approach to get better teaching from this person, but whatever it takes, this is your responsibility.

A principal must evaluate the work of his staff. Although you will want to be friendly and considerate of your staff members, you still must be objective enough to recognize strong and weak points. You cannot let your sympathy for the teacher who has recently lost her husband or your understanding of the person who has poor health stand in your way of making an honest appraisal of his or her performance.

When you are observing your teachers, you should be able

to recognize good teaching when you see it. Strong teachers are often individualistic. They might be unorthodox or eccentric and still very effective as teachers. Also, you should be able to put your finger on the weak spots of the lesson and have constructive suggestions on how these can be corrected.

If you become a principal you must be alert to the new trends in education, and you must make wise decisions as to what changes would lead to the best teaching results. You cannot appropriate an innovation from another school and try to launch it in yours without careful evaluation. Perhaps you'll hear a principal say, "I tried team teaching in my school. It didn't go over." Or "I don't know if flexible scheduling would work. We might try it though." But a good principal analyzes the needs of his particular school and makes improvements rooted in these needs. He lays the groundwork, has pilot studies or tryout periods, and makes certain he will get the support which he needs for the success of the venture before he makes a radical change.

As the head of the school it will also be your responsibility to arrange for workshops and in-service training. In some districts you might have to work out the salary schedule. Also, you will have charge of the testing program of your students, and will need to see that the results are sent on to the proper authorities. You will use the findings from the tests to improve your school curriculum. In many cases you will decide the grading system and report cards to be used.

Your teachers will want you to lead. Staff members feel more secure and function better when they know there is a strong principal at the head of the school. As a high school teacher said, "I always know that Mr. Evans is up there steering the boat. I don't always agree with where we're going, but at least we're headed for a port and not just drifting on the high seas."

So much for your role as an educator. Remember you are also the business manager of a going concern and as such will have a staff under you other than the teachers.

Your staff might be small and consist only of a secretary-clerk, three or four custodians and two cafeteria workers. However, eventually you may be put in charge of a large school with one or two vice-principals, a secretary, registrar, several stenographer-clerks, a telephone operator and a book-keeper. In which case you will also have several custodians to keep your school clean, engineers to run the heating and cooling systems, gardeners for the grounds, security officers, as well as a head cook with many cafeteria workers. To handle this nonteaching or classified personnel requires the ability of a true executive.

As a business manager you will be required to choose equipment for your school, from the cafeteria trays to the latest floor polisher. Also it will be up to you to order such supplies as paper, pencils and art materials and keep an inventory of them. It will be your responsibility to have text-books on hand. You will have to decide how much your plant will be used for community activities; also, who will use it, how often and for what purpose.

There will be special professional personnel who will come and go but be under your jurisdiction while in the building. Such staff members include the nurses, school doctor and those who test for sight, hearing and mental rating.

One of your major functions will be to plan the school budget. You will be required to estimate your enrollment for the coming year and decide how your money will be spent. Some funds will go for capital outlay or permanent purchases. In this area you will have decisions to make such as whether to buy a new piano for the music department or more sewing machines for homemaking. Perhaps it will be necessary to plan additions to the plant or to remodel existing facilities. Much of your budget should be allotted for supplies.

The principal also sets up an administrative calendar for the full year, which includes the opening and closing of school, the change of semesters, sending failure notices, holidays, report card issuance, assembly programs, faculty meetings, teacher rating reports, and all of the other important dates that must be set.

Your school graduation exercises will need to be planned and carried out. A high school principal will receive many student requests for recommendations for jobs and college entrance.

When the dust finally settles at the end of the school year, you will spend a good many hot summer days preparing your annual report to local and state authorities.

Your final role as public relations expert will be equally important. It will be up to you to interpret the school activities to the community. You must "sell" the school to the taxpaying public. As costs of education rise and the taxpayer is bombarded to vote more bonds or to raise the tax limit, it is your task to convince him that he is getting his money's worth.

Unless there is a publicity director in the superintendent's office, you might have to deal with the press. Because the public is interested in the schools, the newspapers give considerable space to them. You will issue reports about enrollment, the instructional program, pupil progress, staff members, building program and P.T.A. meetings.

Student activities, sports and human interest stories get

good coverage, too. Your school newspaper helps to inform the public about your activities. The pupil notices you send home will also serve in this way.

You will be expected to be a leader in your community and to take part in civic affairs. Usually you will be urged to join the service clubs. Frequently you will be called upon to address various organizations to explain or defend your school policies.

Your position as principal will put you in line for promotions to the superintendent's office. A large district has many supervisory positions. You might be placed in charge of guidance or attendance. You might be the director of school planning. Or perhaps you will head the audiovisual department, purchasing and distributing educational films, filmstrips and records.

Large districts have consultants for the elementary and secondary levels. There are department consultants for music, art and industrial arts, positions which might appeal to you. You might have charge of curriculum planning or personnel. The superintendent usually has a director of the budget and business manager as well as several assistant superintendents. Eventually, you might qualify for such a position. And who knows—you might even end up as a school superintendent!

An educator, when asked what qualities made a good principal, said, "Naturally he should have high professional standards and be a leader. He should have good judgment and a sense of fairness. Of course, he should have a real understanding of boys and girls and be able to get along with them. But there is one other quality that is not emphasized enough—he should be able to hold up under stress. If he can't, he'll end up with a nervous breakdown!"

There is a need for both men and women in the administrative field. Qualified members of minority races have many opportunities to serve in this way, too.

As principal of a school you will be like a captain of a ship and have full authority over everything in your school. It will be up to you to steer your course with vision to worthy goals and maximum achievement rather than settling for the mediocre and average. Your strong steady hand at the helm can help both your teachers and your students reach their highest aims.

XIII

Opportunities Overseas

After you have had two or three successful years of experience you might want to try teaching in a foreign land. If you investigate, you will find that there are many opportunities available to the adventuresome teacher.

Jerry Whitaker was just such a person. For five years he had taught eighth grade and boys' physical education in a small-town school in Ohio. For some time he had felt restless and in need of a change.

One noon in early March he was sitting in the faculty room with the rest of the staff. He picked up a professional journal and leafed through it. One article especially caught his attention. He said to the others, "It tells here about teaching in a school for the dependents of the servicemen stationed overseas. That's a great idea! I think I'll try it."

His colleagues thought he was joking. But that night Jerry wrote to the Department of Defense and asked for information. Within two weeks he received a pamphlet entitled "Employment Opportunities for Overseas Educators," along with a preliminary application form. When he studied the pamphlet he found that the armed services have operated elementary and secondary schools for dependents of military and civilian personnel since 1946.

There are about 325 such schools, of which over 200 are

elementary; the rest are junior and senior high schools. These schools have a staff of more than 7,500 professional employees. The total enrollment is approximately 165,000 pupils.

Jerry was particularly interested in the statement on the cover, "American military personnel are stationed around the world. Recognizing the effect on troop morale, the military department permits dependents to accompany their military and civilian sponsors overseas whenever possible. The dependents school program provides for education of minor children. Thus teachers in accepting an overseas assignment are making a direct and important contribution to our national posture."

An applicant could have his choice of the Atlantic Area, Pacific Area or European Area, Jerry noticed. These large areas were broken into twenty-nine smaller ones. One could indicate in what area he would accept an assignment but not a specific city.

After studying the general requirements, which he thought he could fulfill, Jerry completed the application form and indicated he would prefer to go to Europe.

Within two months, Jerry's application was processed and he was asked to go to a nearby military base for an interview.

The interviewer told him, "We provide the dependents with educational opportunities comparable to those in the better school systems here in the United States. Our course of study and all the textbooks used are approved by a committee of experts."

Jerry was pleased to hear that. Then he asked, "What about getting overseas? Do you provide the transportation?"

The interviewer nodded, "Yes, we do."

"How long do I have to stay?" Jerry asked.

"One year. Teachers, librarians, and dormitory counselors

must sign an agreement that they will remain overseas that long. If you were to be a principal the agreement might read twelve, eighteen or twenty-four months."

"Well, that's fair enough."

Jerry signed his agreement and filled out more application forms. Before the school year was over he was notified that he had been assigned to Germany.

Someday, you, too, might want to take part in the dependents school program. The general requirements are:

1. U.S. citizenship.
2. Age of twenty-one years by August 1.
3. Physical ability to perform duties without hazard to self or others; freedom from chronic conditions requiring medical care or medication.
4. Favorable physical characteristics, emotional stability, self-reliance, adjustability, discretion, good morals, socially acceptable personal habits, loyalty to the U.S.A., ability to work successfully with students, parents and school administrators.

You must hold an A.B. degree from an accredited institution and have eighteen semester hours of professional teacher training. If you teach in a special field, necessary preparation for it is required. You must have completed at least two years of successful full-time employment as a teacher, counselor, librarian or school administrator within five years before you apply.

Elementary teachers might be placed in a small school, so they must be willing to teach more than one grade, if necessary. A secondary teacher is often required to teach in more than one subject field, and he also conducts at least one extra-curricular activity.

There are many special teachers assigned for the deaf, hard of hearing, retarded and blind. Librarians, counselors and principals are also employed.

The base pay is about $5,000 with additional salary for advanced education. A dormitory counselor gets an additional $200. A teacher-principal receives about $300 more. The base pay for an administrator is about $7,500 per school year. When available, living quarters are provided at small cost. Sick leave of ten days per year is granted. The dependents school program offers as many opportunities as any other for a foreign assignment.

Patricia Gordon got her overseas experience in still a different way. Patricia was a history teacher in a large high school in Chicago. She was a slim, attractive girl in her twenties, and engaged to a lieutenant in the Air Force who was stationed in Southeast Asia.

One wintry day in January she found a note in her box to report to the principal after school. All day long she worried about whether she was going to "get called on the carpet" for something. Why would the principal send for her? But when she reported to Mr. Langdon, her principal, he acted so friendly that she relaxed.

"Sit down. Sit down, Miss Gordon." He pointed to the chair across from his desk. "Our high school has been invited to participate in a teacher exchange with a school in Manchester, England. A Miss Purcell, who also teaches history, would like to come here for a year. Well, I thought of you. Perhaps you'd be interested in exchanging with her."

Patricia gasped with surprise. "Well, I never thought of such a thing! I—"

Mr. Langdon chuckled. "You don't have to make up your mind just now. But think it over." He picked up a letter. "These are the qualifications. A teacher who participates in an international exchange must be a U.S. citizen, with at least an A.B. degree, and have not less than three years' successful full-time teaching experience, preferably in his subject field."

"So far, I qualify," Patricia said, her cheeks flushed with excitement.

"Above all you have to be a good representative of our country. You must be able to interpret American education and her way-of-life to the English people."

"I could try, anyway."

"I chose you because you are a fine example of a young American woman. You would be a credit to our profession and to our country."

"Why, thank you, Mr. Langdon. I feel very complimented."

"Here is a brochure about the International Educational Exchange Program. As you no doubt know, it is under the direction of the Department of State and the U.S. Office of Education."

As soon as she got back to her classroom, Patricia read through the brochure. She learned that each year nearly 8,000 persons representing 130 countries and territories are exchanged to teach or engage in special study or research.

The exchange program was made possible by the Fulbright-Hays Act, officially called Public Law 87-256, the Mutual Educational and Cultural Exchange Act of 1961. There are six types of exchange arrangements. Some, of course, are two-way: a foreign teacher and an American teacher replace each other. Some are one-way: a teacher comes here from abroad or one goes from here without involving anyone else. Some are summer seminars for foreign language teachers. Other arrangements include no teaching but are for special research and study.

An exchange applicant must have the approval of his school authorities. He must be able to speak, read and write in the language of the host country. He must have good health, moral character, emotional stability, maturity and adaptability. Veterans and persons under fifty are given preference.

In some arrangements a teacher is paid his own salary from his school district; in others he has a maintenance allowance to provide a professional standard of living. Some host countries pay the teacher's transportation; others do not.

Patricia found that she would receive her transportation across the United States and half of her fare from New York to England. She would also get her salary from the Chicago school district.

She accepted the exchange and had a wonderful experience. Many organizations and private people in Manchester entertained her and made it possible for her to learn about life in England. Teachers and others in Chicago were equally cordial to Miss Purcell. The teachers, the schools, the students and the host countries gained in international understanding by this exchange, which is, of course, the main purpose of the program.

Since 1950, UNESCO has undertaken various projects to encourage international exchanges and study between members of the teaching profession. UNESCO means United Nations Educational Scientific and Cultural Organization.

UNESCO administers fifty travel and study grants per year as well as teacher exchanges. However, most of the exchanges are at the college level. This organization also recruits teachers for universities abroad.

Michael Gomez, a Mexican-American, who taught Spanish in a junior high school in San Diego, California, always wanted to do something to further better relations between the United States and Latin America. Mike was bilingual. He had been reared in the outskirts of San Diego by his Mexican parents. He had an understanding of both American and Mexican ways of life.

Mike was married to a Mexican-American girl who was an elementary teacher. Maria was also an entertainer and had considerable experience in radio and television work.

For a long time Mike kept looking for the right place where both he and his wife could be most useful. Finally he wrote to the Chief of the U.S. Information Agency in Washington, D.C.

It wasn't long before Mike received literature about the Binational Centers which the U.S. Information Agency maintains abroad. There are Binational Centers in all the principal cities and in many smaller communities of the other American republics. There are also centers in twelve cities in the Near East, ten in the Far East and two in Europe.

The purpose of the Binational Center is to explain the institutions, government and the way of life in the United States to the people of the host country. This information is given by lectures, on radio broadcasts, through study groups and in special courses. The center has a library with books from the United States. The library provides a lending service as well as a reference one.

Both Mike and Maria were hired by the U.S. Information Agency and were sent to Ecuador. They taught about twenty hours a week on all levels from elementary to more advanced work. Since the majority of students were adults, most of their classes were held in the evening. Both of them took part in the radio broadcasts.

Besides their classes in English, they taught courses that presented phases of American cultural heritage, history, literature, art and music. Sometimes they worked with special groups such as businessmen, doctors, lawyers or engineers.

The Binational Centers throughout the world perform many services for private and government organizations. They act as a clearinghouse for applications for scholarships to universities in the United States. The recipients of the scholarships are given an orientation course in the Center.

The Centers need librarians, people with TV, radio or newspaper experience, as well as teachers. To be on the staff of a Center one must be a U.S. citizen, and have spent his early formative years in the United States. He must be in good physical condition.

An A.B. degree from an accredited college is another requirement. An employee has to be able to speak the language of the country to which he is assigned. His pay will run between $6,000 and $15,000 per year.

A teacher in a Center must have had professional training and at least one year's experience. The age limits are between twenty-three and forty. A teacher must agree to stay for at least two years.

The Peace Corps offers another way to have an overseas experience. Most of the work in the Corps is a form of teaching, although professional training is not a requirement.

An applicant for the Peace Corps must be at least eighteen years of age and be a U.S. citizen. Married couples are eligible if they have no dependents.

Applicants are required to fill out a volunteer questionnaire which is available at any post office. Before assignment, they must take a noncompetitive Peace Corps placement test.

Volunteers receive enough reimbursement to provide for food, housing, clothing and incidentals besides getting an allowance of $75 a month and must be willing to serve two years, which includes an eight- to ten-week training period.

The Overseas Educational Service is an agency which recruits professors for universities in Asia, Africa and Latin America. The OES finds teachers for the U.S. Agency for International Development in the AID program.

The OES-recruited personnel are expected to serve a minimum of two years. There is a great variation in salary, which might range from $5,000 to $10,000 a year.

The International Cooperation Administration, or ICA, uses advisors in fifteen fields, one of which is education. The ICA advisors work closely with the people and governments of host countries to carry out broad programs to improve conditions. A tour of duty in this agency is also for two years.

Another group, the Asian-English Teaching Project, wants male teachers for two-year assignments in Cambodia, Japan, Korea and Taiwan.

Private companies, such as the major oil organizations, sometimes hire teachers for schools for dependents of their American personnel stationed abroad. Since there is no clearinghouse for these positions, application must be made directly to the company involved.

There are positions available in the schools in the U.S. territories and possessions. There are agencies that recruit for independent schools in foreign countries. Also many religious and missionary groups need teachers for mission schools on all levels.

Teaching overseas can be an interesting and worthwhile experience. However, before you attempt it, you should have a genuine interest in cultures different from your own. You should sincerely want to learn about other people.

You should realistically face the fact that there are many frustrations in overseas service. Sometimes the climate is too hot, too dry or too humid for a person from a temperate zone. Housing might be uncomfortable and medical care inadequate. Sometimes you will find the delays in getting things done most irritating. You might even experience some anti-Americanism.

However, for the teacher who is genuinely interested in other people and who can adjust easily, a year or two of overseas service would be the adventure of a lifetime.

For further information contact the following:

Teaching in Overseas Dependents Schools

International School Services
147 East 50th Street
New York 22, New York

or

Department of Defense
Washington, D.C.

Exchange Teachers

Teacher Exchange Section
International Exchange and Training Branch
Bureau of Elementary and Secondary Education
U.S. Office of Education
Washington, D.C. 20202

or

Exchange of Persons Service
UNESCO
Place de Fontenoy
Paris 7 e, France

Teaching in a Binational Center

Chief
Personnel Services Staff
Office of Personnel and Training
U.S. Information Agency
Washington, D.C. 20547

Peace Corps

Office of Public Affairs
Peace Corps
Washington, D.C. 20525

Aid Program

Executive Director
Overseas Educational Service
522 Fifth Avenue
New York, New York 10036

To Be an ICA advisor

International Cooperation Administration
Office of Personnel
Washington 25, D.C.

Private Companies with Schools for Dependents of Overseas Personnel

Foreign Commerce—Foreign Policy Department
Chamber of Commerce of the United States
1615 H Street N.W.
Washington, D.C. 2006

Teaching in the U.S. Territories and Possessions

CANAL ZONE	PUERTO RICO
Personnel Director	Secretary of Education
Panama Canal Company	Department of Education
Balboa Hts., Canal Zone	Hato Rey, Puerto Rico

PACIFIC ISLANDS
Director of Education
Trust Territory of the
    Pacific Islands
Truk, Caroline Islands

GUAM
Director of Education
Agana
Territory of Guam

AMERICAN SAMOA
Director of Personnel
Pago Pago
American Samoa

VIRGIN ISLANDS
Assistant Commissioner
    of Education
Department of Education
St. Thomas, Virgin Islands

Agencies Recruiting for Independent Schools

International Schools Services
147 East 50th Street
New York 22, New York

or

2000 P Street N.W.
Washington, D.C.

African-American Institute
345 East 36th Street
New York 17, New York

or

1234 Twentieth Street N.W.
Washington 6, D.C.

Teachers for East Africa
Teachers College
Columbia University
New York 27, New York

Asian-English Teaching Project (men only)
Asia Foundation
105 Market Street
San Francisco 5, Calif.

Religious and Missionary Groups Recruiting for Mission Schools

COLLEGE
United Board for Christian Higher Education in Asia
150 Fifth Avenue
New York 11, New York

ELEMENTARY AND SECONDARY
Commission on World Missions
475 Riverside Drive
New York 27, New York

American Board of Commissioners for Foreign Missions
14 Beacon Street
Boston 8, Massachusetts

The Protestant Episcopal Church
National Council Office
Church Mission House
281 Park Avenue, South
New York 10, New York

American Friends Board of Missions
Executive Secretary of Friends World Committee
152A North 15th Street
Philadelphia 2, Pennsylvania

American Lutheran Church
Board of World Missions
Executive Director
422 South Fifth Street
Minneapolis 15, Minnesota

Professional and Technical Workers
Aliyah for Israel
515 Park Avenue
New York 22, New York

XIV

Teachers Who Touched the Stars

No book about a career in teaching would be complete without citing some famous teachers. Down through the centuries there have been hundreds of them. Let's consider a few. How about Martin Luther, John Milton, Woodrow Wilson and Lyndon Johnson?

"Now, wait a minute!" you protest. "Of course, those are all famous names. But—"

Well, they were teachers, too.

During your preparation to become a teacher you will take a required course in the history of education and will learn about many great educators whose influence on schools is still felt today. Such names as Locke, Pestalozzi and Froebel will become familiar ones. But think of names you already know. You will find that many of them are teachers who touched the stars.

One of the greatest teachers of all times was Socrates who lived in Athens from 469 to 399 B.C. Socrates was a stonemason and carver by trade who wandered about the streets barefooted, wearing a smock. He had good manners, but he was an ugly man and was neither polished nor aristocratic.

Socrates talked with everyone. He loitered on street corners and questioned shopkeepers, soldiers and travelers. Each afternoon he went to the gymnasium where young men exercised and old men bathed in the sun. He asked questions of the men in the gymnasium and let them do most of the talking. He questioned the famous citizens of Athens as well as the obscure ones; he said he knew nothing and was trying to find out.

Through his keen and penetrating questions and his ability to steer the conversation, he revealed his brilliant mind. He convinced his fellow Athenians that thought alone was one of life's strongest forces. He said he was a tutor who trained people to think. He compared himself to the athletic coach who does not run or throw the javelin but teaches others to do it better. Many young men became his followers and studied his philosophical teachings.

Socrates' pupils proved that he was a great teacher. His most eminent one was Plato (427–347 b.c.), a rich and gifted nobleman who established a college named Academy to carry on the philosophical studies of Socrates. Plato carefully selected the students for his Academy through entrance examinations. In fact, Plato was the founder of the examination system. Plato was also a superb wrestler. Perhaps he was one of the first educators to stress physical education in school. Plato devoted much of his life to writing books on philosophy, in which he recorded the conversations of Socrates and his followers.

One of Plato's students was Aristotle (384–322 b.c.), the son of a wealthy doctor, who entered the Academy when he was seventeen and remained for twenty years. After the death of Plato, Aristotle left Athens. Soon he took charge of the education of the young Macedonian prince who later became Alexander the Great. Aristotle taught the young prince to appreciate and cherish Greek civilization. Later when Alexander conquered so much of the world, he spread Greek civilization wherever he went.

When Alexander set out upon his Asiatic conquests, Aristotle, then fifty, returned to Athens and opened a school called Lyceum. His Lyceum resembled a modern college in the sense that both teaching and research went on. The advanced students worked in small seminar groups. Aristotle combined lectures and class discussion for his younger pupils. His courses were organized to survey a subject. He took each topic and broke it down into a number of problems so that his pupils could discover concepts through their own efforts. His presentation was the forerunner of a modern college course.

The great religious leaders—such as the Jewish prophets, Buddha, Jesus of Nazareth, and Mohammed—were all outstanding teachers, of course. But one religious figure who had a great impact on schools as such was Martin Luther (A.D. 1483–1546). The Reformation destroyed the authority of the Roman Catholic Church over the schools in the states that followed Luther. The educational system of many areas was thrown into chaos.

It was Martin Luther who advocated education for people at large and not just for aristocrats and churchmen. He stressed the need for schools that would prepare people for everyday life as well as giving them a firsthand acquaintance with the teachings of the Bible and catechisms. Too, he emphasized the need of teaching music in schools.

Martin Luther stressed the fact that the state was obliged to provide schools for all children and should compel attendance to them. He helped in founding these schools and insisted on the education of girls as well as boys. He believed that if a city could spend large amounts to build roads and fortify itself, it should spend a like sum on schools. The prosperity of a city, he pointed out, does not consist in strong walls, treasures and great houses but in capable, honorable and well-educated citizens.

Although education at home was important and should be continued, he believed, it was too narrow and there should be schools maintained at public expense so children could "gather within themselves the experience of all that has happened since the world began."

Over four hundred years ago Luther also wrote, "If magistrates may compel their able-bodied subjects to carry pike and musket and do military service, there is much more reason for them compelling their subjects to send their children to school. For there is a far worse war to wage with the devil, who employs himself secretly in injuring towns and states through the neglect of education." The colonists who came to America brought Martin Luther's ideas on education with them.

As you study *Paradise Lost* and *Paradise Regained* remember that the immortal poet John Milton (1608–1674) was a teacher at one time. For seven years he had a school for boys from wealthy and aristocratic families.

Besides being a poet, and a secretary to Oliver Cromwell, Milton was a noted pamphleteer and letter writer. A series of letters to a friend was published in 1644 as the *Tractate of Education.*

Milton believed that education was to fit a man "to perform justly, skillfully and magnanimously all the offices private and public, of peace and war." He believed that knowledge comes to a learner through his senses, and periodically a person should examine his knowledge to give it solidity and organization. Unlike Luther, he saw no reason to waste time and money on educating girls.

In his tractate, Milton described an ideal school called an

"academy" that should be held in "a spacious house and ground about it, big enough to lodge one hundred and fifty persons." He believed that boys from twelve to twenty-one should attend the academy, and he worked out a comprehensive curriculum appropriate for them.

That description of an academy and its curriculum helped to inspire a new type of educational institution in England. Many academies for boys were started. Later, in America, Benjamin Franklin advocated that academies be founded, and the first one was opened in 1751. Soon, others were established throughout the colonies.

Another name undoubtedly familiar to you is Horace Mann (1796–1859). Perhaps you have attended a school named after him. Mann was born in Franklin, Massachusetts, and was educated at Brown University and Litchfield Law School. From 1823 to 1837 he served in the Massachusetts State Legislature. During that time he was instrumental in the enactment of laws for decent treatment of the insane and for reform in prison and jails. He worked to prohibit the sale of lottery tickets and alcoholic beverages. Through his efforts a state board of education was established, the first of its kind in the United States.

In 1837, Horace Mann was appointed secretary to the board of education and began a battle for school reform that lasted during his lifetime. In a few years, he modernized the schools of Massachusetts, raised the standards and salaries of teachers, and did away with corporal punishment in the classroom. He established three normal schools to train teachers, which were the first in the nation. He not only brought on reform in his own state but all over the country, and in doing so stirred up an outcry of criticism. He fought all of his critics and ushered in a new era of education.

William James, the eminent psychologist, lived from 1842

to 1910. He was the brother of Henry James, the novelist. William was educated at Harvard University and for many years served on its medical faculty. Sometime in the middle seventies (the exact date has been lost) he began experiments that mark the birth of experimental psychology in the United States. In 1890, his monumental book *The Principles of Psychology* brought him world fame and is now considered a classic. He also rose to eminence as a philosopher and taught both philosophy and psychology at Harvard.

The philosophy of James was continued and developed by John Dewey (1859–1952), who was a professor of philosophy at the Universities of Minnesota, Michigan and Chicago. While at the University of Chicago, he was director of the School of Education and established an experimental school. He emphasized that pupils learn "by doing." His principles of education had a profound influence on the development of American education and brought about the progressive schools.

One of the most famous teachers in America, Anne Sullivan Macy (1866–1936), unconsciously practiced the principles of John Dewey in her work with Helen Keller.

Anne Sullivan was born in squalid poverty in Massachusets to an Irish immigrant family. Because her eyesight was failing she was sent to the Perkins Institution for the Blind in Boston and learned the manual alphabet and how to read by means of her fingers. She had a meager education and no teacher training. After two operations her eyesight improved and she was hired to tutor Helen Keller, then six years old. The work of Anne Sullivan with young Helen Keller has been immortalized in the play and movie *The Miracle Worker*.

Helen Keller learned to speak and to read braille. She wrote on a special typewriter. She was graduated with honors from Radcliffe College and went on to gain world fame as an author and lecturer. She devoted her life to helping other handicapped persons. None of these achievements would have been possible without her teacher, who stayed with her until her death in 1936.

One of the most outstanding teachers that Princeton University ever had was Woodrow Wilson (1856–1924). Some authorities claim that he was one of the greatest teachers of his century. He was a professor of jurisprudence and political economy at Princeton from 1890 to 1902, when he was elected to the presidency of the university.

He was a tall noble man with great energy and intelligence. Among other things, he was an avid sports enthusiast. When he first came to the university there was no football coach. His first year at Princeton found him rushing away from his classroom to work out with the football team. For ten weeks he acted as coach and whipped the team into the best condition he could.

However, it was his courses that brought him fame. His pupils described him as the finest lecturer they had ever heard. He had a brilliant mind, a rare gift of mimicry, and a delightful sense of humor. More than once his students stood and cheered him at the end of one of his illustrious lectures.

Many prominent men in the government today have come from college faculties. For example, Dean Rusk was an associate professor of government at Mills College, in California, from 1934 to 1938. Hubert Humphrey speaks of himself as a refugee from the classroom. In 1941, he taught at the University of Minnesota and then became Superintendent of Teaching of the WPA's Workers Education Service. He was a professor of political science at Macalester College, in St. Paul, in 1944.

It is common knowledge that Lyndon Baines Johnson attended Southwest State Teachers College at San Marcos, Texas, with every intention of becoming a teacher. While he was going to college he needed money, so he applied for a limited teaching certificate and took the academic year 1928–1929 to teach fifth, sixth and seventh grades in a little town called Cotulla.

Johnson is still remembered in Cotulla as the teacher who brought about better relations between the Anglo and Mexican children in the school. As strapped as he was for money, young Johnson used his first salary check to buy athletic equipment for the Mexican boys.

At the end of the school year Lyndon Johnson returned to college and completed his studies for a bachelor of science degree in 1930. He became a speech and history teacher at Sam Houston High School in Houston. He also was the debate coach, and his team won the county, district and state championships in the spring of 1931. Johnson then became the secretary to the newly elected Senator Richard Kleberg, and went to Washington, D.C., in 1931. Thus another fine teacher was irrevocably lost to the classroom.

As you read about famous people who were teachers you will note that they brought to their classes the same dedication and same enthusiasm that later won them eminence in other fields. Some of the greatest men in history have been teachers. Many of the most important advances in civilization have been brought about, not by generals or politicians, but by teachers. In education you will find a profession worthy of the best in you.

Bibliography

BOOKS

Administering Library Service in Elementary School, by Jewel Gardiner, American Library Association, Chicago, 1954.

The Adolescent Years, by William W. Wattenberg, Harcourt Brace & Co., New York, 1955.

The American College and University, by Frederick Rudolph, Alfred A. Knopf, Inc., New York, 1962.

The Art of Teaching, by Gilbert Highet, Alfred A. Knopf, Inc., New York, 1950.

The Beginning Teacher, by William A. Yauch, Martin H. Bartels, Emmet Morris, Holt Publishing Co., New York, 1955.

Better Libraries Make Better Schools, Anthology Selected by Charles L. Trinkner, The Shoe String Press, Inc., Hamden, Connecticut, 1962.

Chance and Choice in Higher Education, by M. M. Chambers, The Interstate Printers, Danville, Illinois, 1962.

A Commitment to Youth, Edited by Abraham S. Goodhartz, Bookman Associates, New York, 1960.

The Community College Movement, by Ralph Fields, McGraw-Hill Book Co., New York, 1962.

Concise History of Education, by Herman Weimer, Philosophical Library, New York, 1962.

Curriculum in the Modern Elementary School, 2nd edition, by Robert Beck, Walter Cook, Nolan Kearney, Prentice-Hall, Inc., Englewood Cliffs, N.J., 1960.

Democratic Processes in the Secondary Classroom, by Rosalind M. Zapf, Prentice-Hall, Inc., Englewood Cliffs, N.J., 1959.

181

The Education of American Teachers, by James Bryant Conant, McGraw-Hill Book Company, New York, 1963.

Education of Exceptional Children and Youth, by William M. Cruickshank and G. Orville Johnson, Prentice-Hall, Inc., Englewood Cliffs, N.J., 1958.

The Education of Teachers, by G. K. Hodenfield and T. M. Stinnett, Prentice-Hall, Inc., Englewood Cliffs, New Jersey, 1961.

An Educational History of the Western World, by Adolphe E. Meyer, McGraw-Hill Book Company, New York, 1965.

The Effective School Principal, 2nd edition, by Paul B. Jacobson, William C. Revis, James D. Logsdon, Prentice-Hall, Inc., Englewood Cliffs, New Jersey, 1963.

Exceptional Children, by Florence L. Goodenough, with the assistance of Lois M. Rynkiewicz, Appleton-Century-Crofts, Inc., New York, 1956.

The First Year in School, by E. R. Boyce, James Nisbet and Co., Ltd., London, England, 1953.

Foundations for Elementary School Teaching, by Robert B. Norris, Herbert G. Tag, Doris E. Nason, Richard F. Neville, The Ronald Press Company, New York, 1963.

Helping Counselors Grow Professionally, by William Evraiff, Prentice-Hall, Inc., Englewood Cliffs, New Jersey, 1963.

Helping Handicapped Children in School, by Edward William Dolch, The Garrard Press, Champaign, Illinois, 1948.

Higher Education and the Human Spirit, by Bernard Eugene Meland, University of Chicago Press, Chicago, 1953.

The History of Education, by Ellwood P. Cubberley, Houghton Mifflin Co., Boston, 1948.

The History of Western Education, 7th edition, by William Boyd, Barnes and Noble, Inc., New York, 1965.

Introduction to Exceptional Children, by Harry J. Baker, The Macmillan Co., New York, 1953.

Legal and Ethical Responsibilities of School Personnel, by Warren E. Gauerke, Prentice-Hall, Inc., Englewood Cliffs, New Jersey, 1959.

Living in the Primary Grades, by Clarice Dechent Wills and William H. Stegeman, Follett Publishing Co., Chicago, Illinois, 1956.

Luther on Education, translation by F.V.N. Painter, Concordia Publishing House, St. Louis, Missouri, 1889.

Lyndon B. Johnson, by Harry Provence, Fleet Publishing Corp., New York, 1964.

Modern Elementary Curriculum, by William B. Ragan, Holt, Rinehart, & Winston, New York, 1960.

Modern Methods in Elementary Education, edited by Merle M. Ohlsen, Henry Holt and Company, Inc., New York, 1959.

Modern Methods in Secondary Education, revised edition, by Jean D. Grambs, William J. Iverson, Franklin K. Patterson, Henry Holt & Company, Inc., New York, 1958.

Modern Secondary Education, by William M. Alexander and J. Galen Saylor, Rhinehart & Co., New York, 1960.

New Directions for the American University, by Frederick Mayer, Introduction by Aldous Huxley, Public Affairs Press, Washington, D.C., 1957.

Opportunities in Teaching Careers (paperback), by Benjamin Fine, Vocational Guidance Manual, Universal Publishing and Distributing Corporation, New York, 1963.

Organization and Conduct of Guidance Services, by Lester D. Crow and Alice Crow, David McKay Co., Inc., New York, 1965.

Patterns of Primary Education, by David C. Davis, Harper and Row, Publishers, New York, 1963.

Practices and Trends in School Administration, by Emery Stoops and M. L. Rafferty, Jr., Ginn & Co., Boston, 1961.

The Revolution in the Schools, edited by Ronald Gross and Judith Murphy, Harcourt, Brace & World, Inc., New York, 1964.

School Health Services, Publication of the Joint Committee on Health Problems in Education of the National Education Association and the American Medical Association, edited by Charles C. Wilson, M.D., Washington, D.C., 1964.

School Teaching as a Career, by James R. Boylan, Henry Z. Walck, Inc., New York, 1962.

Secondary School Administration: Problems & Practices, by Ivan H. Linder and Henry M. Gunn, Charles E. Merrill Book, Inc., Columbus, Ohio, 1963.

Selection for Secondary Education, by J. J. B. Dempster, Methuen & Co., Ltd., London, England, 1954.

The Smaller Liberal Arts College, by Lewis B. Mayhew, The Center for Applied Research in Education, Inc., Washington, D.C., 1962.

So You're Going to Be a Teacher, by Robert L. Filbin and Stefan Vogel, Barron's Educational Series, Inc., Great Neck, New York, 1962.

Student Teaching, by Raleigh Schorling, McGraw-Hill Book Company, New York, 1949.

Teacher—Anne Sullivan Macy, by Helen Keller, Doubleday and Company, New York, 1955.

Why Teach?, Anthology edited by D. Louise Scharp, Henry Holt & Co., New York, 1957.

Woodrow Wilson, Life and Letters, by Roy Stannard Baker, Doubleday, Garden City, New York, 1927.

BOOKLETS, REPORTS AND PAMPHLETS

Blueprint for Tomorrow . . . Today, Covina-Valley Unified School District, Western Regional Center, Educational Facilities Laboratories, Inc., School of Education, Stanford University.

Carnegie Corporation of New York Quarterly, October 1961, Vol. IX, No. 4.

A Design for the Administration of Public Education, by George D. Strayer, Educational Administration, Monograph No. 1, School of Education, Stanford University.

Designs for Education 1963, A Report from School Planning Laboratory, Western Regional Center, Educational Facilities Laboratories, Inc.

The Education of Teachers, A summary of discussions from National Commission on Teacher Education and Professional Standards, Conference held at San Diego State College, California, 1960.

How to Be a Pro, by Sylvia Brotman, Special Assistant, The National Education Association, Washington, D.C., 1958.

Improving the School Environment, by Raymond C. Schneider and Jon S. Peters, The School Planning Laboratory, Stanford University.

An Interim Report, School Construction Systems Development, Educational Facilities Laboratories, New York.

Invitation to Teaching, National Commission on Teacher Education, National Education Association, Washington, D.C., 1966.

Lifting Standards of Preparation, Department of Classroom Teachers and Research Division, National Education Association, Washington, D.C., 1956.

Planning for Schools with Television, Prepared by Dave Chapman, Inc., Industrial Design, for Educational Facilities Laboratories, New York, 1960.

Research Résumé—Factors Related to Success of Beginning Teachers, California Advisory Council on Educational Research, No. 19, May 1961.

School Scheduling by Computer—The Story of GASP, Educational Facilities Laboratories, Inc., 1964.

The Schools and Urban Renewal, A Case Study from New Haven, A Report from Educational Facilities Laboratories.

Schools Without Walls, Profiles of Significant Schools, Educational Facilities Laboratories, Inc.

Should You Be a Social Worker? by Russell W. Ballard, Reprint —New York Life Insurance Co., 1958.

Spectrum of Electronic Teaching Aids in Education, Educational Facilities Laboratories, New York.

Teaching Abroad, Occupation Information Bulletin Number Two, Career Counseling Unit, Ann Arbor, Michigan, 1962.

A Window to the Future, Report of the 1964 Airborne Institute for Community College Planning.

PERIODICALS

Accreditation of Teacher Education, by G. W. Denemark, *Educational Leadership,* Vol, 22, April 1965, pages 458–60.

The Brookhurst Plan, An Experiment in Flexible Scheduling, by Elayne B. Hofmann, *N.E.A. Journal,* Vol. 54, No. 6, Sept. 1965, pages 50–52.

Changing Curriculum of America's Schools, by John I. Goodlad, *Saturday Review,* Vol. XLVI, No. 46, Nov. 16, 1963, pages 65–67, 87–88.

Concerns for Children Everywhere, Elementary Education in To-day's World, by Alice Miel, *Childhood Education*, Vol. 37, No. 2, pages 61–64.

Cultural Unity and Diversity in New States, by C. C. Moskos, Jr., and W. Bell, *Teachers College Record*, Vol. 66, No. 5, May 1965, pages 679–94.

Learning Patterns in Secondary School, by B. F. Brown, *Secondary Education*, Vol. 40, No. 5, May 1965, pages 195–200.

Library Science in the High School, by Sylvia Zisking, *School Library Journal*, Vol. 8, No. 6, February 1962, pages 14–16.

State Certification or Else, Review of Certification in Education, by L. B. Kinney and J. C. Stone, *C.T.A. Journal*, Vol. 60, No. 3, May 1964, pages 12–13.

Team Teaching, by David W. Darling, *N.E.A. Journal*, Vol. 54, No. 5, pages 24–25.

The Launching Pad, by Sarah M. Bush, *Delta Kappa Gamma Bulletin*, Summer 1962.

Index

ABOUT THE AUTHORS

Dorothy Dowdell was born in Reno, Nevada and spent her early childhood there and in Carson City. In her teens she moved with her parents to Northern California and attended high school in Roseville. After graduation she moved to Sacramento, which has since been her home. She attended the University of California at Berkeley where she graduated with an A.B. degree. After graduation she was married and went with her husband to Germany where he studied for his Ph.D. When her children reached junior high age, Mrs. Dowdell completed her teacher training at Sacramento State College and taught in the elementary schools for fourteen years.

Joseph Dowdell was born in San Francisco, California. The Dowdells moved across the bay to Marin County where he spent his childhood. He decided to be a teacher while attending the University of California, at Berkeley. He holds an M.A. degree from Stanford University and an M.S. from the University of California. Dr. Dowdell was a laboratory assistant in botany at the University of California for two years, and also a teaching fellow at Stanford University, Palo Alto. He was a science instructor at the Sacramento City College for thirty years. Dr. Dowdell has now retired to write, travel and enjoy his family.